It's the *Jobs*, Stupid

It's the *Jobs,* Stupid

E.A. Madden

iUniverse, Inc.
Bloomington

It's the *Jobs*, Stupid

iUniverse books may be ordered through booksellers or by contacting:

iUniverse
1663 Liberty Drive
Bloomington, IN 47403
www.iuniverse.com
1-800-Authors (1-800-288-4677)

ISBN: 978-1-4620-2143-7 (sc)
ISBN: 978-1-4620-2144-4 (hc)
ISBN: 978-1-4620-2145-1 (e)

Library of Congress Control Number: 2011907506

Printed in the United States of America

iUniverse rev. date: 06/17/2011

Dedication

To my Mother, one of many millions of Americans who go to work every day and hold this nation together.

Those who can not remember the past,
are doomed to relive it.

-Santayana

Acknowledgment

To Mitch McConnell and John Boehner.
Without you, I never could have found the courage to write this book.

It's The Jobs, Stupid

Introduction

It probably won't come as any great surprise that politicians lie to us. They lie all the time. They lie about little things. They lie about big things. They lie when the truth would do, always looking toward the next election, always trying to manipulate the passions of the electorate to garner a few more votes, always trying to paint the other political party as evil. Once elected or reelected, they sell their congressional votes to the highest bidders which, in virtually all cases, are the biggest corporations with the deepest pockets.

So this book is about truth-telling. And facts, big, bold, in-your-face, red, white and blue facts that anyone with a computer and access to a search engine can verify for himself. And blame. Blame is good. If we don't learn anything from our mistakes, what's to stop us from making the same mistakes over and over again (which, in fact, we have). And solutions. Since an old military friend suggested that a soldier should never present a problem unless he is also prepared to offer a solution, part of this book is devoted to just that: solving the problem.

It's tough to make facts and figures entertaining, especially numbers. I mean from zero to nine there's only ten digits. How exciting can it get? So I tried to keep the numbers to a minimum wherever I could.

I am positive you will find things in here that you absolutely hate and reject. I hope you also find a few things that have the ring of truth about them. That's where our conversation as Americans can begin.

It is so sad that we're scared to death to talk to each other, except maybe to our immediate family, about our views on economic, governmental, or environmental issues even though an honest exchange of creative ideas is desperately needed at this time in history. Suppose I espouse one opinion to a co-worker and it's the exact opposite of what he believes? Things could get pretty tense between us and even worse if the boss happens to agree with the other guy's position. So we avoid conversations which could morph into testy remarks even though a sincere dialogue about our economic plight and what to do about it could become a learning experience and a chance to expand our options, for both of us. No wonder sports, music and Hollywood celebrities dominate our social conversations. They're safe subjects. They're also totally meaningless to our ability to make the rent payment or the mortgage payment every month.

Nothing of any significance changes in these fifty United States unless a huge number of people come together to form a critical mass. 111 million people tuned in to watch the 2011 Super Bowl, an historic record. The country was just as bad off economically after the Super Bowl as it was before it but at least for a brief moment we came together as Americans to cheer for our teams. We didn't question whether the individual players were Democrat or Republican, Methodist or atheist, we just wanted our team to win. You and I are also playing on a team. It's the American team and we're playing against the rest of the world to win the global economy war. For us and our kids and our grandkids, it's the only war that matters. The last thing we need is for members of our American team to get into arguments over who's more conservative or more liberal or more patriotic. What we do need is a coming together to form that critical mass of purpose to make good things happen.

"Every kingdom divided against itself is laid waste, and no city or house divided against itself will stand." (Matthew and Luke)

We are all Americans. We're all in this together, like it or not. So let's look at our national situation in new ways. Let's beat the politicians and the money changers at their own game. Why just reform the system when we can redesign the system from scratch? We'll look at the past to see what worked and what didn't but not too much past because we Americans are forward-thinking, progress-oriented. This country wasn't built by playboys and dilettantes who were afraid to get their hands dirty and it won't be destroyed by them either. We, the American people, are absolutely undefeatable once we set our minds to a common goal. It is this strength that we must draw on now. It is o.k. to be angry about our current economic situation as the Teabaggers are. Anger can be very energizing. But let's use that anger to seize control of our lives and build something brand new, not to attack our fellow citizens because they happen to belong to a different political party. That's not the American way and nothing good or wholesome can come of it. It is more likely to spark violence than to spur progress, something the politicians are too ignorant to understand even though it is they who have caused this widening chasm between us with their lies.

Finally, this book is most especially addressed to our future, our curious young adults who may have not quite decided on their politics. Older Americans have pretty much staked out their turf as either conservative or liberal and most are not likely to be swayed one way or the other. Young Americans are more likely to still be undecided, and it is you who have the most to lose or gain from our country's direction in the future. You are very busy, I know, whether you have a job or are looking for a job and you may believe politics has nothing to do with you. The truth is, politics has everything to do with you. Political decisions are the reason you may be unemployed or under-employed. And for way too long, we have paid little or no attention while the politicians gave the whole farm away. This book is going to show you how to get the farm back. We will provide some perspective on events that may have happened before some of you were born and some context for the seemingly insurmountable mess we're in now. There is a way out but before we can solve the problems we must name them, something the politicians are working hard to prevent us from doing.

Contents

V. Parting Shots

Appendices

Noblesse Oblige

Taken from the French, the literal translation is "nobility obliges" or more to the point, with privilege comes responsibility. In the moral sense, the philosophy came over on the Mayflower with our European heritage which posits that the fortunate, well-off upper classes have a duty to help the poor, down-trodden lower classes and to serve for the common good. Princess Diana's two sons, William and Harry, both served their turns in the military as did their father, Charles, following a long, British tradition. Royalty, most especially, is bound to this obligation of service. All of our American institutional charities have evolved from this concept of giving and serving.

So too has the idea that society's privileged bear the greatest burden in crisis, especially war. In this vein, when Harry Truman (1945-53) took office during World War II, the top marginal tax rate (See Chapter 29 for full definition) stood at 94 percent of individual income and we needed every penny of it. It financed the war. It was lowered to 91% during Dwight Eisenhower's (1953-61) eight years in office. The income rate upon which the top marginal tax rate applied was $400,000/year, a lot of money in those days. Come to think of it, it's still a lot of money compared to the average American wage today. During John Kennedy's three years in office (1961-63) the tax rate stayed at 91%.

When Lyndon Johnson took office (1963-69) he was able to lower the top marginal tax rate to a low of 75.25 percent but he did it by also lowering the top tax threshold to $200,000. In other words, people making 50% less money had to pay more in taxes to make up for the shortfall in revenues caused by the lowering of the top marginal tax rate.

During the terms of Richard Nixon (1969-74) and Gerald Ford (1974-77) the top marginal tax rate ranged from a high of 77% to a low of 70% and stayed at 70% throughout the office of Jimmy Carter (1977-81).

Now we arrive at a point of critical departure in the history of our modern economy. The presidency of Ronald Reagan (1981-89) was marked by a dramatic decline in the top marginal tax rate from 69.125% to 28% over his eight years in office. More startling were the top incomes to which the rate applied: $171,000 to $106,000 to $90,000 in 1987, to $29,750 in 1988. In other words, he turned the concept of noblesse oblige on its head.

At the same time, Reagan announced that we would shift the main emphasis of our economy from manufacturing hard goods, to the information sciences. We would off-shore the production of routine products to free up Americans for the coming service-centric economy. At that time, even though I was the beneficiary of the largess of the Department of Defense, I asked myself how Reagan's proposition could work. Would we all stand around with our hands in each others' pockets and sell insurance to each other? Coming from a blue collar background myself, I wondered how a country that doesn't make anything could long survive. I didn't know then how prophetic my concerns were. Ronald Reagan's tax policies were the beginning of an economic decline that has continued and accelerated right up to today resulting in the savaging of the American wage earner and the pillaging of the average American taxpayer. (We'll deal with the Clinton presidency and others, a little later and show how they were a continuation of Reagan's policies, not a departure).

Humpty Dumpty

Alan Greenspan would have felt right at home. Our former fed chief is famous for coining the phrase, "irrational exuberance" before the pop of the dot.com bubble in 2000. So too does the phrase apply to the lead-up to the crash of 1929 and the aftermath of wide-spread depression and 30% unemployment. The stock market was pretty much unregulated in the 1920's and there was the promise of making a fortune to anyone willing to invest. Investors didn't always have to have all the money to pay their way in. 10% buy-ins, known as "buying on margin" were common. Many investors borrowed money from banks to buy stocks. As the market climbed higher and higher, more and more investors were enticed into the buying frenzy. By 1929, $8.5 billion had been lent to investors on margin, an astonishing amount of money considering that the entirety of the U.S. paper money in circulation did not equal that much. Banks had free rein over their depositors' money and could use the funds to make speculative investments for their own accounts in the stock market.

It began to unravel. In a grossly overvalued market, industry was over-producing and inventories continued to build. As the market declined so too did the sales of goods. Prices came down, sometimes steeply, but since workers were being laid off by the thousands, sales dropped still more and corporate earnings fell along with their stock prices. The stock market began to sell off. Brokers who had billions in loans on the street started to call in their margins but investors could not meet the calls and were forced to sell their stocks at a loss. The market responded with a bigger sell off. (Starting to sound familiar?) A spiral of selling set in. The market crashed on October 27, 1929. Banks failed. Lay-offs reached into the millions. Farm properties, which had been struggling for many years to make a profit, hit auction blocks by the thousands.

President Hoover (1929-1933) a conservative Republican, believed a public dole would do more harm than good. He favored private charities and local governments as a way to provide help to the homeless and unemployed. Homeless camps sprang up all across the country. There was no federal safety net back then. People were starving. Local governments tried to help. Everywhere, bread lines appeared. Cities started to buckle under the weight of caring for the populace with steadily falling tax revenues. Suicides increased. By the year 1930, 5000 banks had failed and there was still no end in sight. Hoover ultimately tried to persuade congress to enact business-saving legislation but it was far too late. So many banks were failing that they would not allow depositors to withdraw money. State governors had to force banks to take "holidays" to prevent a total collapse of the banking system. Fully one-third of the labor force was unemployed. Into the chaos of 1932, Franklin D. Roosevelt was elected. He carried forty-two states.

Remembering F.D.R.

Franklin Delano Roosevelt epitomized the concept of noblesse oblige. Roosevelt himself came from the privileged classes of American society but he chose to throw his lot in with the common man. He would later call the Republicans "dupes of the economic royalists". FDR embraced the responsibilities of the office with confidence and firm resolve. When he took the White House at the beginning of 1933, we were in the midst of a deep, entrenched depression, our unemployment rate was over 30%, and our national economy had essentially collapsed brought on by the excesses of Wall Street and the banking industry. At his inauguration, Roosevelt made his famous speech, "The only thing we have to fear is fear itself…" and promised he would recommend legislation to lift the economy from the ground up emphasizing the important role each citizen was to play. (President Roosevelt's inaugural speech is included in its entirety as Appendix C to this book.) The challenges he faced as he assumed the presidency are so similar to our recent financial crisis, the speech could have been written and delivered in 2008. The body of his sweeping reforms came to be known as the "New Deal" and earned Roosevelt accolades from historians as one of the three greatest presidents in all of American history.

Roosevelt set about to reestablish stability and to seed the regrowth of the broken system. On the day after his inauguration, he ordered all the banks closed and they were to remain closed until congress could enact regulations to govern them. Then he immediately called for a special session of congress to address the banking crisis. In short order, congress passed the "Emergency Banking Relief Act" which gave the President broad powers to regulate bank transactions and specified the conditions by which banks could reopen. They had to establish that they were solvent, as judged by federal inspectors. Many smaller banks were placed into conservatorship until they could demonstrate that they were well enough to fully reopen.

In quick succession, numerous laws were passed by congress to reform the banking and stock market sectors. The Glass-Steagall Banking Act was passed in 1933 just months after Roosevelt took office. One of the most important provisions was to separate depositors' banks from investment banks and forbid commercial banks from dealing in speculative financial activities such as the stock market. It was thought that this type of risky practice helped in large part to bring about the Crash of 1929. (The law was essentially unchanged until 1999 when it was repealed. Eight years later, we had our own crash in 2007). In addition, the 1933 act set up the Federal Deposit Insurance Corporation which guaranteed individual deposits up to a specified amount. Congress also established the Securities and Exchange Commission for the mandatory registration of all publicly traded securities and licensing of brokers. The Public Utility Holding Company Act was passed in 1935 to prevent unregulated monopolies and price manipulation in the utility industries such as in electric power generation.

The Tennessee Valley Authority, also established in 1933 with the urging of President Roosevelt, was a very successful experiment in regional planning and development. It provided for the building of dams, generation of power, soil conservation, crop rotation, flood control, reforestation and the revitalization of industry over an eight-state area in the southern U.S.

FDR also signed into law in 1933 the "Buy American Act" which required the U.S. government to buy U.S.-made products to keep American economic resources in America. The law also extended to local, indirect purchases which used federal funds, such as interstate highways and other infrastructure projects. Although this law was very useful and productive when first established, it has been repeatedly weakened over the years with so many exceptions and loopholes it's been rendered meaningless. The list of countries which qualify for "exception" encompasses all of the industrialized world and many emerging market countries.

The centerpiece of FDR's programs was the social security system which provided old age, survivors' and disability insurance and unemployment compensation. This program remains in effect today and is taken for granted by average Americans.

On behalf of a gravely injured citizenry, Roosevelt instituted the C.C.C. (Civilian Conservation Corps) to provide gainful employment to young men between the ages of 18 and 25. The government hired and paid these men directly to help save our natural resources. They worked all over the country planting trees, fighting forest fires, and building roads and bridges. They accomplished so much and the program was so successful that it ran from 1933 until 1942 when we joined the war in Europe (World War II).

FDR also established the (P.W.A.) Public Works Administration to construct public buildings and various infrastructure projects such as dams. The P.W.A. let contracts to private construction companies and also loaned money to local governments for similar projects. One of the most successful and long lasting is the Tennessee Valley Authority (see above).

Established in 1935, the National Youth Administration enabled poor high school and college students to continue their education by providing part-time jobs.

President Roosevelt put his trust not in the banks and corporations that got us into that mess and caused the crash of 1929 and the ensuing depression, but in the strength and resilience of average American citizens. He vowed to rebuild the country from the bottom up, not the top down, using the ultimate unit of industrial power, the American worker. The purpose of these work programs which were designed to be temporary was to get people gainfully employed so they could spend their paychecks back into the economy, increasing demand for products, which would stimulate business, which would result in hiring more workers and so on and so on. Such are the dynamics of a vital capitalist system. And such are the ethics of a noble president and a responsible congress that they believed it was their duty to act on behalf of the American people. Noblesse oblige.

That was a very long time ago.

One More Trip To The Reagan Ranch

Our intent here is not to present a blow-by-blow history lesson, but to discuss the creation and destruction of jobs in our system of government so let's fast-forward to the economic policies of Ronald Reagan (1981-89).

President Reagan was a nice guy and very popular with the electorate. He possessed the easy grace and relaxed style that came from his many years in the professional film and television industries before he became governor of California. Reagan was a conservative president who believed in smaller government and reduced marginal tax rates. It was the centerpiece of his administration. During the eight years of his presidency, he reduced the marginal tax rate from a high of 70% to a low of 28%. He also reduced capital gains taxes while loosening government regulation of the economy and he increased the tax rate on new investment which had the effect of encouraging off-shoring of our manufacturing base in conjunction with Reagan's preference for an "information technology economy" as noted in Chapter 1.

Reagan's stated aim was to reduce government spending so he could reduce taxes. As anyone who has been on this earth for more than twenty years can testify, government spending never decreases. It has a life-force all its own. To demonstrate the point, the federal government spent 27.9% of national income in 1980, Jimmy Carter's last year as president and Nominee Reagan attacked Carter's free spending. But by 1988, Reagan's spending had increased to 28.7% of national income. And tax cuts simply increase the federal deficit. The money to run the government and contribute to state infrastructure has to come from somewhere. If the American citizens can not or will not pay their own way, we have to borrow the money from somewhere and "renting" money costs money as anyone who uses a credit card knows only too well.

Following in more detail is the economic legacy of the Reagan administration which set the stage for the continuing excesses of the next three presidents, all of which have led directly to the mess we're in today. I liked Reagan and voted for him both times. But just because we like someone, it is not sufficient reason to vote for that person as President of the United States. Voting is not a popularity contest. You must do what I did not do at the time, research the candidate's positions on the issues, especially economic issues.

Reagan's eight year administration is the only one in modern presidencies not to have raised the minimum wage. It stayed at $3.35/hour throughout his presidency. Soon after Reagan took office, he reduced the maximum tax rate which had a very positive effect on the very wealthy and as a result, increased the national debt from 33.3% of gross domestic product (GDP) in 1980, to 51.9% at the end of 1988. We started to borrow heavily from overseas. In 1985, we began our trade deficit with China at $6 million dollars. The national debt, which stood at $700B in 1980 rose to $2.8 trillion during the Reagan presidency. We had been the world's largest creditor after World War II. Ronald Reagan turned us into a debtor nation and we have never recovered.

We might think that the dramatic drop in the top marginal tax rate would result in a huge surge in investment but such was not the case. Between Jimmie Carter and Reagan, the gross domestic product hardly budged and actually dropped significantly under George H.W. Bush who followed Reagan.

Reagan grew the government too in the form of defense spending which rose from 4.9% of GDP at the beginning of his presidency to 5.8 to 6.0%

of GDP (gross domestic product) during his term in office. (The Vietnam War had ended in 1975 and we were in one of the rare periods where we were not fighting with anybody.) Nonetheless…

Another negative of Reagan's tax policies was the Tax Reform Act of 1986 which as a by-product, retargeted the "alternative minimum tax" to tax payers of more modest means, i.e. the middle class while leaving the richest tax payers unscathed.

The most glaring effect of "Reaganomics" is that from 1980 through 1988, the share of total income going to the richest 20% of families grew from 44.1% to 46.3% while the poorest 20% saw their share of income decrease from 4.2% to 3.8% during the same years. Real wages of average workers declined sharply (adjusted for inflation) just as the very wealthy saw their incomes soar. Perpetual Christmas for the rich. Ironically, the country's productivity where Reagan expected huge gains actually slowed to less than that of his predecessors, while real tax receipts declined. The savings rate declined during the Reagan years as well, a pretty good indicator that average families were having more and more trouble in making ends meet. We know all about that. We've been overextended on our credit cards for years, until we had our own Great Recession of 2007-09.

We don't know how Reagan proposed to grow the larger economy. He never said. But we do know how his policies affected us over-all. The folks who already owned vacation homes and multiple luxury cars got to buy their first yacht. The super rich got to buy a bigger yacht and perhaps a small island somewhere. The vast majority of Americans who earned more modest incomes got to pay higher taxes and struggle mightily to save up a down-payment to buy their first home or replace an aging auto or pay college tuition. They also dined at McDonald's a lot.

Many people, mostly Republicans, still say that the way to raise tax revenue is to cut taxes because they say, tax cuts encourage investment. And it does work. Somewhat. In the short term. But it turns out, as psychologists have demonstrated, that any positive change in incentives will have a positive effect in the short run but it is due to the novelty of the change, not the change itself. Over time, people tend to take for granted the incentives they are receiving, viewing them as entitlements, so you have to continually extend more and more tax cuts to "goose" investment. And at some point, investors will simply move their money someplace else where the profits are richer which, in fact, they have.

In his 1980 campaign speeches, Reagan vowed to return the economy to the principles in vogue before the Great Depression. We should have known we were headed for trouble then. The unregulated, debt-laden, supply-side economic policies popular before F.D.R. are precisely what caused the crash of 1929 and the Great Depression which followed it.

As Reagan prepared to leave office at the end of 1989, our trade imbalance with China had risen to over $6 Billion U.S. Dollars.

A Zero Sum Game

Let's look at the results of President Reagan's conservative economic policies in a slightly different way.

Think of a cherry pie. Now cut it into equal pieces. A basic nine inch pie will yield eight pieces, one piece for each of eight guests. But Bob wants two pieces and so does Jim. And when you, the host, turn away, Bob and Jim each steal a third piece. The remaining two pieces are simply too small to divide among the remaining six guests, so you give Bob and Jim the last two pieces of pie. The pie is gone and the other six guests go home without dessert. That is a somewhat tedious, but accurate, description of a zero sum game.

In game theory as well as in economic theory, zero-sum refers to a scenario where, in order for one player to win, the other player must lose. Chess is a zero sum game; one winner, one loser. One variation on the concept is if the total gains of the players are added up and the total losses subtracted, they will equal zero; hence, a zero-sum game. Cherry pie = (4 + 4 - 8 = 0).

The world's total wealth is a finite number. It's a huge number to be sure but it's not infinite. If the world's total wealth represents 100% and I possess 90% of it, your share can not exceed 10%.

Warren Buffet, one of the richest men in the world, famously stated that he pays less in taxes (16%) than his secretary does. That's because the rich have tax deductions you and I don't have and they are able to shelter their incomes under multiple corporate structures where they get to deduct/depreciate everything from real estate to foreign taxes to bad investments to paper clips. And because the world's economy is a zero-sum game, if the rich pay less in taxes, you and I have to pay more. The money has to come from somewhere.

We can't just casually print up a couple of trillion dollars. It has a devastating effect on inflation and currency values. We can borrow the money as we have been doing, mostly from China. But money costs money. In the not too distant future, the debt will exceed 100% of our gross domestic product. In short, our current fiscal trajectory is unsustainable. We are about to go over the cliff.

In the months since I wrote this brief vignette, I've been genuinely surprised at how many times TV's talking heads have used the "zero-sum" phrase in the negative, as in, "It's not a zero-sum game" in describing our economy. Interestingly, those talking heads have usually come from the titans of the business community hoping to defend their off-shoring of so many American jobs. My response to them is this: It depends on how big your world is. When you're talking about world economies as we are here, yeah, it really is a zero-sum game.

Dorothy And Prescott's Boy

George Herbert Walker Bush (1989-1993) was neither our best president nor our worst (we'll get to his kid later). Billed as a conservative, he still managed to sign into law the "Americans with Disabilities Act" and reauthorized the "Clean Air Act". He fought to increase federal spending for education, childcare and technology research. Most notably, Bush was concerned about the $220 Billion deficit left to him by the Reagan administration (three times its size since 1980) and he favored a combination of spending cuts and tax increases which theoretically, would have reduced the deficit over five years. To his credit, in raising taxes, Bush was trying to do the responsible thing and insert some sanity into Reagan's runaway deficit. After a congressional battle, the Democratic majority won the right to increase the marginal tax rate, but not by much, just 3% to 31%. Keep in mind that during some of our country's most productive years, the top marginal tax rate hovered between 90% and 70%.

Bush was also the American sponsor of the "North American Free Trade Agreement" (NAFTA) although it was not signed into law until after he left office. Bush, together with Canadian Prime Minister Brian Mulroney, partnered the talks which were to remove most tariffs and trade restrictions between the U.S., Canada and Mexico. A key provision was the removal of most investment restrictions between the three countries. Guess which citizens and companies had the most dollars to invest? There were also no safeguards to protect labor rights or the environment.

There are many people on both sides of the NAFTA issue, for and against. I am on the against side. Yes, the new agreement stimulated our economy.

For awhile. Just imagine all the engineers, all the advisors, all the architects, all the new computers we had to buy, all the software we had to write, all the international contracts we had to prepare, all the new factories we had to build in Mexico, a few in Canada…American investors were falling all over themselves to throw money at Canada and especially Mexico, where labor was dirt cheap. Funny thing is we could have just as easily invested those same dollars in upgrading our own factories here at home and the stimulation to our own economy would have been permanent not temporary as these off-shoring schemes turn out to be. So in order to obtain a measly 3% increase in the top marginal tax rate, we had to sacrifice our labor base and our capital investment base to a country with an average income of a couple of dollars a day. At the same time, Bush signed the Immigration Act of 1990 which increased legal immigration to the U.S. by 40%.

Remember Ross Perot? He was the billionaire who ran for president as an independent against both Bush and Bill Clinton and he gave both of them heartburn. Perot was in favor of balancing the budget, in favor of increasing taxes and against NAFTA. Perot's most memorable quote was, "That giant sucking sound you hear is jobs leaving the U.S. and heading for Mexico". His on-again, off-again candidacy managed to rack up 19% of the popular vote for president, one of the highest totals for a third-party candidate in U.S. history, so apparently, some Americans were paying attention.

But we can't overestimate the power of our two entrenched political parties. In acquiescing to the tax increase, Bush lost the support of his Republican base (the party that has never seen a nickel it didn't covet for itself) and was defeated by Democrat Bill Clinton in 1992, and by 2004, our trade deficit with Mexico and Canada, stood at $111 Billion, twelve times its size before NAFTA.

Slick Willie

"Slick Willie" was the nickname given to Bill Clinton (1993-2001) during his first term as Governor of Arkansas by a critical newspaper editor. The nickname resurfaced during his run for the presidency in 1992. One thing is for sure, President Bill Clinton defied easy characterization. He was charismatic and inscrutable. His policies were in turns both liberal and conservative. He was good for the country. He was bad for the country. Maybe some of Ross Perot did rub off onto Clinton. But not the best part.

As an aside, it is so sad that Clinton spent most of the eight years of his presidency being investigated by a special prosecutor and grand jury at the instigation of the Republican Party for alleged fraud in the Clintons' investment activities in Arkansas. The special prosecutor could find no wrong doing in Clinton's financial affairs but did manage to catch him in a lie regarding his sexual escapades, much to the public humiliation of his family, a new low in our national discourse. And unfortunately, in our new era of "gotcha politics" that bar just keeps getting lower and sleazier with every election.

But moving on, Bill Clinton did reach out to America's modest income families with the Earned Income Tax Credit which incentivized the working poor to keep working, rather than go on welfare.

Clinton also signed into law the State Children's Health Insurance Program (CHIP) which expanded insurance coverage to approximately six million children through federally funded grants to states. And he signed the Family and Medical Leave Act and the Minimum Wage Increase Act.

On a more conservative note, Clinton initiated and passed through congress a major welfare reform bill in 1996. This bill eliminated (theoretically) the welfare system.

But it is for the passage of the Gramm-Leach-Bliley Act signed in 1999 that conservatives appreciate Clinton. This act repealed the financial safeguards of Roosevelt's Glass-Steagall Banking Act, in place since 1933, which prohibited commercial, depositors' banks from making risky loans and engaging in speculative financial ventures, such as securities trading. Now the commercial banks, investment banks, securities firms, insurance companies and brokerage houses were all free to engage in each others' businesses, merge, expand, acquire each other and get much, much bigger and they did just that, to become the Thirty-Trillion- Dollar-Colossus called "Too Big to Fail" and dwarf the tax revenues of the federal government by 2007, just eight short years later.

Clinton was a deficit hawk and he proposed raising taxes on the richest 1.2% of Americans in his budget proposal. The Republicans in congress fought him tooth and nail to prevent this really puny tax increase. Every Republican in both houses voted against the increase. The budget package passed by one vote in the senate (Al Gore's) and two votes in the house. And as a result of that tax increase, the country experienced a significant decline in the budget deficit and by 1998, the nation achieved a budget surplus, the first surplus since 1969.

Bill Clinton was an early and enthusiastic champion of free trade so it was not surprising that he eagerly signed NAFTA (the North American Free Trade Agreement) proposed by his predecessor, George Bush, (the elder) and in 1994, it became law. Clinton believed that NAFTA would increase U.S. exports and create new American jobs. But alas, Ross Perot was proven right. After the initial flurry of activity getting the Mexican and Canadian ventures up and running, the factories, the jobs, the income and the tax revenue moved mostly south to Mexico where labor was the cheapest.

And Clinton wasn't done yet. Next, he held meetings with the twelve Pacific Rim countries and arranged an agreement to gradually remove trade barriers. Then the White House participated in trade negotiations with the forerunner of the World Trade Organization, known at that time as the GATT (General Agreement on Tariff and Trade). These were slightly less successful but Clinton's trade agreement with China was passed by congress in 2000 and as Bill Clinton prepared to leave office in 2001, our trade deficit with China had reached $83,096 Million dollars.

The Law Of Supply And Demand

The Law of Supply and Demand is a construct of economics that says that when supplies of goods and services are plentiful, prices tend to drop; when supplies of goods and services are scarce, prices tend to rise. The principle has been around since at least the nineteenth century and is today one of the fundamental concepts of economics. The law predicts that price will move toward the point that equalizes the quantities of goods or services with supply or demand. The four components of the law are:

- If the demand for a commodity increases, but the supply does not increase equally, the price will increase.
- If the supply of a commodity increases, but the demand for that commodity does not increase equally, the price will decrease.
- If the demand for a commodity decreases, but the supply does not decrease equally, the price will decrease.
- If the supply of a commodity decreases, but the demand does not decrease equally, the price will increase.

We can easily apply the law to our own employment situation and other aspects of our stagnant economy. As more and more jobs are sent overseas, jobs available here at home become more and more scarce. With so many candidates to choose from the employer can easily find someone willing to work for less pay. So we see that as the available supply of employees increases, the demand (wages) tends to drop. One of the most recent polls on labor statistics indicates that for every job opening in the U.S. there are 5.5 potential applicants. This ratio fluctuates and has been as high as

6.25 applicants per job. Smaller paychecks mean smaller taxes which erode federal and state tax revenues as well as causing real pain to our nation's working poor.

An influx of twelve million illegal aliens over a short time span who will work for almost nothing and pay no taxes further erodes the tax base while taking advantage of the money available for government services like education, health care (especially for their American-born off-spring), policing, etc. There's nothing quite like twelve million fertile immigrants to distort the law of supply and demand, further depressing wages. And don't think because you have a college degree you are exempt. The Law of Supply and Demand applies across the board and depresses everyone's wages. It's in the numbers not in the education.

Then there's our boutique wars, which are a continuous drain on our economy. There's only so much money to go around for infrastructure so while we rebuild the infrastructures of the various countries we fight with, our infrastructure rots. But chin up. We're providing handsome profits to the military/business complex of corporations who champion these wars to congress. What about the taxes the corporation pays? The fact is, businesses pay considerably less in taxes, proportionately, than you do. All those deductions, don't you know. And according to the Department of Treasury's own web site, "Individual tax payers contribute five times the tax dollars as do business taxes". Yes, we citizens really do most of the heavy lifting in our economy not the mega-bucks corporations. A recent case in point: General Electric Company (GE) which reportedly paid no federal income tax in 2010, yet had a $14 Billion Dollar profit. We'll look into GE's corporate profile in more detail a little later.

Supply and demand. There is just so much supply of money to go around while the demand grows exponentially. The price of money is very, very high indeed.

A Bird In The Pot Is Worth
Two Of The Bushes

George W. Bush (2001-2009) dragged his feet on the issue of illegal immigration for all of his eight-year presidency saying that "they are just doing the jobs Americans don't want to do" and enabled as many as one million illegal immigrants per year to cross into the U.S. from Mexico. In recent years, Mexico has served as a pipeline for illegals also coming from South and Central America.

Bush enacted tax cuts which mostly benefited the rich. In 2001, he introduced his plan to cut taxes in the amount of $1.35 trillion a year, one of the largest tax cuts in U.S. history, repeating the well-worn Republican mantra that the tax cut would stimulate the economy and create jobs. There was a sunset clause written into the law at that time which was to return the tax rates to their pre-2001 level in ten years, meaning 2011.

By October 2008, our long-term national debt had risen to $11.3 trillion dollars (The debt had been $5.6 trillion in 2000, the start of the Bush presidency). The poverty rate increased from 11.3% in 2000 to 12.3% by 2006. Median family income dropped by $1175 between 2000 and 2007 (adjusted for inflation). Unemployment was at 7.2%.

Starting in 2007, the U.S. entered the worst recession since before World War II, a recession which still plagues us today in the form of slow growth and continuing unemployment/underemployment, situations which are probably permanent given the large-scale off-shoring of so many formerly American jobs.

After the attacks of September 11, 2001, Bush embarked on an invasion of Afghanistan where Osama bin Laden the 9/11 mastermind was known to be hiding. We quickly toppled the Taliban regime but bin Laden alluded us. Inexplicably, Bush turned his attention away from Afghanistan and invaded Iraq which had nothing to do with the attacks on our homeland. To date, the Iraq war has cost our country over one trillion dollars, 4400+ American lives and continuing problems with a crooked and unstable government in Afghanistan. *Osama bin Laden remains at large.

Other random facts about the Bush presidency which may or may not be well known include the fact that the cost of the Iraq war was not included in the Federal Budget of the United States until Barack Obama came to the White House. Bush also pushed for free trade world-wide and starting in 2005, our trade deficit with China reached $202,278 Million dollars.

In the following two chapters, we will look at several issues made more costly and more deadly by the ideological tunnel vision of the Bush administration.

---

*   On May 1, 2011, Osama bin Laden was captured and killed in a Pakistani suburb, providing long delayed justice to the American people.

If It's 2012, It Must Be Somalia

Korea, Vietnam, Iraq, Afghanistan and many, many smaller skirmishes in between, we never actually finish the war, we just move it to a different country.

War is good for business, a fact that is well known in Washington, D.C. circles where I once hung my hat. It's not just the guns, it's the new uniforms, the MRE rations, the communications gear of all kinds, the blankets, the soap, and probably a few rubber duckies for the homesick kids. It's the multi-billion dollar aircraft systems and the nuclear submarines. It's the billions and trillions of lines of computer code that guide these systems as well as the missile systems which seek their targets. It's the lavish American embassy we built in Iraq with a cost topping out at close to 600 Million U.S. Dollars.

The problem is, making war is one of the pursuits which is articulated in our Constitution with powers designated specifically to the congress and to the president: "The Congress shall have the power to declare war…to raise and support armies…to provide and maintain a navy…" "The President shall be Commander in Chief of the army and the navy of the United States…" and these two branches of government have used their powers over the military extensively and repeatedly to reach a variety of political, economic and even personal objectives, not always to benefit the security of the American people. And quite often, not to preserve the lives and limbs of America's citizen-soldiers.

In truth, although Roosevelt's efforts in the 1930's jump-started a dead economy, it was World War II which finished the job of getting us out of the depression. That's because manufacturing shifted into high gear to produce the enormous quantity and variety of goods we needed to fight the war. New factories were built but most impressive, many existing factories were retrofitted from making consumer goods to mass producing war supplies. The spirited will and fellowship of the American people during that war is legendary. We were united coast to coast in our determination to defeat our enemies, Germany and Japan. Almost as an afterthought, our economy took off and for decades, gave the U.S. the greatest prosperity the world has ever known. World War II was a just war and our participation was unavoidable at that time in history.

However, we can not start another war every time the country has an economic decline, although there are politicians who try really hard to do exactly that because, as already stated, it's good for business. Yes, it may goose the economy in the short term but it is not a viable long term solution to economic malaise because ultimately, it just runs up more long term federal debt.

We've been dipping into the Social Security Trust Fund for decades to finance the War du Jour by Republican presidents and Democrats alike and those payroll taxes are not progressive. They hit lower and middle income taxpayers disproportionately. Higher bracket wage earners max out from paying the payroll tax each year at a rather measly $106,800 gross salary, even if their earned income is in the millions and even if they light $100 bills instead of candles and yes, they do receive social security benefits when they retire even if they live to be 100. Maybe if the government had kept social security receipts in a "lock box" as Al Gore once recommended, social security would not be on life support as it is now.

But getting back to Somalia, aside from running a very profitable enterprise from piracy, Somalia's primary threat is in destabilizing the countries surrounding it. Then of course there's Iran, pretending not to be building nuclear weapons capability. China has started saber-rattling and it's making some of its neighbors very nervous. So many enemies to choose from. So little time. These countries will just have to get in line if they want to fight with us. We haven't wrapped up Iraq and Afghanistan yet. And we've had troops in South Korea and other countries around the world since the end of WWII. Now would be an excellent time to start invoicing these countries for the military protection we've been providing for the last 60+ years including to our former enemies, Japan and Germany.

Then there's world-wide Islamic terrorism. Has the threat gone away? Absolutely not. We live in a world full of malevolent malcontents who are religious fanatics or mentally deranged or both who hate the industrialized countries because it is easier to blame them for everything than to take responsibility for their own lives. There have always been evil people but today's world-wide instantaneous communications have enabled the most vicious, anti-mankind specimens among us to find each other and join forces as easily as we can put a softball game together. And they are endlessly resourceful. Our biggest mistake is that we continue to underestimate the goals and determination of the terrorists even after the horror of 9/11. Some have said we need to try to understand why the terrorists hate us; start a dialogue with them so we can change their attitudes. Horse crap. People believe what they want to believe. They accept facts selectively, integrating those facts that bolster their beliefs and rejecting facts that contradict their point of view. The terrorists are no different in that regard than anybody else. No, we can't change the terrorists. We have to change us.

But our government is stuck in a 20th century battlefield mentality and the Iraq war was the consequence of that mismatched logic. We were attacked on 9/11 by devotees of Osama bin Laden. Nobody disputes that, not even the Bush administration. So what did we do? Instead of staying in Afghanistan and hunting down bin Laden and his goons with cadres of special forces, we attacked another country, Iraq, and toppled a head of state using tanks, troops and heavy artillery. Instead of fighting the war visited upon our home land, we mounted the kind of war we're comfortable in fighting. Shock and awe, remember? 20th century mentality. We have got to stop trying to win WWII all over again. It's a different world now. Move on.

In 1960, Soviet Premier Nikita Khrushchev took off his shoe and slammed it against his table at the United Nations while ranting "We will bury you!" and the world trembled in fear that he might. The U.S. responded with a massive build-up of nuclear and conventional weapons. The ensuing arms race ultimately bankrupted the Communists and toppled their government from within. But that was then and this is now. We can't win this war by throwing yesterday's solutions at today's problems. What good will it do to deploy a multi-billion dollar missile defense system if a nuclear arsenal can be carried into the country in a suit bag?

We must re-think everything. We need to be making our fighting forces smaller, lighter, faster, quieter, better trained in urban and guerilla warfare, quick insertion and extraction techniques, small independent units with specific limited missions, with much better human intelligence on the ground and the ability to infiltrate terrorist cells. The 21st century soldier must be every bit as agile, flexible and adaptable as the terrorist he faces. Middle-aged teachers from Dubuque and paunchy bankers from Rome, Georgia (though incredibly patriotic) just won't cut it. It's time to start rebuilding and reconfiguring a dedicated military force that is trained to address the unique challenges posed by this new enemy.

We should be training more people to speak Islamic languages and actively recruiting foreign operatives to work with our domestic people. Much of our overseas clandestine activities were greatly scaled back after the collapse of the old Communist regime. We've never needed those "human intel" resources more. We need operatives stationed in every country around the globe. Lots of them.

The U.S. electronic surveillance program, another left-over icon of 20th century warfare, is not well suited to picking up terrorist conversations. To begin with, it throws a very wide net over billions of snippets of conversations. It's much more likely to pick up phone sex than a pair of plotting Al Qaeda. Besides, the terrorists are on to us regarding electronic surveillance so they use foot messengers and arrange face-to-face meetings to do their plotting. We need ears in-country.

We need to actively incentivize our young computer nerds to focus less on creating new video games and gadgets and more on the serious technology of identifying bombs and biological weapons hidden in cargo and suitcases.

Ten years after the attack on the U.S., our continued lack of ability to detect weapons is mind boggling. Where is our government's sense of urgency? Where is the outrage of the American people? Why can't we get our kids' heads out of their iPods long enough to understand that this is a real war and they are about to inherit it? In our preoccupation with Iraq and Afghanistan we are being drawn further and further away from the very real and increasing threat to our security, international terrorism.

And now it's even closer than that with the discovery of our own home-raised terrorists. Terrorism is a movable feast don't you know, so why should we continue to send the same few brave men and women back into the foreign maelstrom until we succeed in killing them? To what purpose? The casualness with which presidents and congress commit our young citizens to the battlefield is astonishing. It reminds me of the old saw, "Let's you and him fight; I'll hold your coat". It is our government, of course, gallantly holding the coats while our citizens, our sons and daughters wade into the fray. You politicians can't have it both ways. Bring back the draft or bring our sons and daughters home alive and well, not in broken pieces, not in bloody body bags. I would go one better. If I were president I would force congress to make a formal declaration of war, something we have not done since World War II, before committing our kids to another "police action" or whatever slick name they're calling these military misadventures now.

Shock and awe. What a bunch of crap. It made me wince the first time I heard the phrase from the Bush administration right before we invaded Iraq. How incredibly arrogant. There is much wisdom in the Teddy

Roosevelt military school of thought; "speak softly and carry a big stick". If these wars are important enough to fight, they are important enough to rally the whole country. Don't tell Americans to "go shopping" as George W. Bush did while a few of the brave spill their guts in the earth of Iraq and Afghanistan. It even sounds monstrous to just say it. What must our troops think and feel, those who manage to make it home alive to the triviality of daily living in these United States? To the country that is all but oblivious to their injury and suffering and loss?

Back in 1961 as President Dwight Eisenhower prepared to leave the White House after serving eight years, he warned about the potential excesses of the "military-industrial complex" and the marketplace tendency to make swords instead of plowshares for the glory, profit and power of waging war. Eisenhower knew full well of that which he spoke. He was the Supreme Commander of the Allied Forces, which defeated Germany on May 8, 1945 and Japan on August 14, 1945, ending WW II.

Se Habla Espanol

Guilt-tripping. The Democrats are famous for it. If the Republicans have never seen a nickel they didn't covet for themselves, the Democrats have never seen a vote they didn't covet, even if they have to give the country away to get it. Common sense should inform the Democrats that American citizens have real, legitimate anxieties about our de facto open border policy with Mexico. But no, if we protest that we're just trying to protect our own families, our jobs, our heritage, then of course, it must prove we're racists. If we say we don't know who is coming across our border, it could be terrorists, we're racists. If we're anxious about the drug wars, the human trafficking, the increasing threats and intimidation to American citizens and American law enforcement...racists.

It is disingenuous to equate the very real racial discrimination against our African-American citizens as the same racism as toward Hispanics. Refusing to serve Black Americans at a lunch counter is racism. Setting up separate public facilities for blacks and whites is racism. Educating children separately by race is racism. Our black citizens have been part of the fabric of our country since its founding when many of them were forced to America against their will. To suggest that our attitude toward Hispanics is "racism" is to deny the very real and painful discrimination experienced for many years by our African-American citizens.

This is not racism. This is a battle for economic survival in a scarce-resource world and we are losing it.

Americans might be surprised to learn that our uninvited guests easily find work in the U.S. (94% nationwide) as delivery men, cooks, house cleaners, nannies, gardeners, and supermarket stockers with no papers, no I.D. of any kind. They are forced to work long hours, have no labor protections and pay no taxes. They also are paid sometimes half of the legal minimum wage. They live in slum apartments, two and three families to a unit. If this is not quasi-slave labor than I don't know what is. Yet the illegals' continuing residency here has the protection of the federal government. Nobody can touch them. Nobody can challenge their right to be here. The authorities just look the other way. Any attempts by local or state governments to get the situation under control, as in Arizona, are immediately quashed by the feds. There have been federal laws on the books for many years requiring resident aliens to carry I.D. on their persons, but when local authorities try to enforce the law, they are promptly blocked, again by the feds, who show no intention of taking up the responsibility. Americans see this Catch 22 situation and they seethe, given the ever-shrinking pool of jobs. When people can't find jobs they take to the streets, to drugs and to crime which is exactly what is happening in cities all across America. We already have over two million people in our prisons. How many more prisons can we build? And who is going to be left with a job to support them? All because the rich and connected of the country, including politicians, demand cheap, tax-free labor to make their beds, and care for their kids and landscape their gardens. And yes, the politicians (especially Democrats) who believe it is more important to chase Hispanic votes than to ensure a level playing field for the livelihoods of American-born citizens.

The politicians have been telling us for more than ten years that the Mexicans and other Hispanics are just "doing the jobs that Americans don't want to do". This argument is ringing increasingly hollow as the unemployment rate has soared and stubbornly refuses to decline.

Americans would do those jobs, gladly, if the jobs paid a living wage. The dirty little secret in our country's history is that our economy has always been based largely on quasi-slave labor, first the blacks, then women, now

Hispanics from impoverished countries. Nobody can live on the federal minimum of $7.25/hour when a loaf of bread costs $1.99. And neither can the illegals. After forcing their way into this country they may pick crops for a season or two then they head to the cities where they compete for jobs against Americans who have worked and paid taxes for generations. The net result is so much more damaging to the average American's economic status than the elitist politicians want us to understand.

Many Americans don't earn enough wages to afford health insurance, even if they still have a job. No surprise, neither do the illegal aliens. If they get sick or have an accident they go to the emergency room of the local hospital where they can not pay for the services received. Those costs in the end are passed back to you and me in the form of higher medical bills and insurance premiums. Name any service you can from health care to education to law enforcement to child services, accommodating the needs of such a large, illiterate and indigent population increases the costs of the average American taxpayer at the same time that wages are decreasing in real terms by competition from that very same group and the on-going off-shoring of American jobs. We are destroying the middle class, the primary engine that drives our economy and our democracy.

Culturally, we have always welcomed new blood to our shores and we should continue to do so; new immigrants add new ideas, a fresh perspective, renewed energy. We have assimilated peoples from all over the world; Irish, Italian, Baltic, Indian, Spanish, Asian and we've been all the richer for it. In one way or another, we are all immigrants.

But this immigration is different from any immigration that has come before it.

What's changed? In the U.S. every succeeding wave of newcomers has had to learn English and learn it quickly if they were to survive economically in their new homeland. And we provided no special language assistance to the Italians, the Germans, the Yiddish, the Chinese, the Poles or any other group who migrated to this country. They had to make it on their own. Hey, it built character and showed us what they were made of. Gradually, these newcomers also blended into the "American way" of doing things and adopted our culture. But this time around, the people who are breaching our southern border are not interested in being assimilated. They come for the jobs not because they want to join the larger society. While they send money to their families back home, they continue to retain their culture, their language and their national identity and they demand that we adapt. So we find that there are multiple Spanish language TV stations in every city, Spanish language radio and countless newspapers and magazines in Spanish. Spanish words have even begun to creep into English language TV broadcasts. Our government panders for Hispanic votes by offering official publications in Spanish, while our utility companies, credit card companies and countless other commercial businesses helpfully offer assistance in Spanish. While most of the world seems to be adopting the English language as the most commonly-spoken second language around the globe, we in the U.S. seem to be going in the opposite direction.

So today, the Mexicans and other Hispanics are setting up a dual society within the U.S. with their own language, their own culture, they're own heritage and because of their much higher birth rate, native English-speakers will soon become the minority in a Latino-centric culture.

I feel a profound sense of betrayal by my government in the lack of urgency to secure our border and reestablish our sovereignty as a nation. The huge number of illegals arriving in such a short time feels like an invasion not an immigration. And we have gone from an exclusively English-speaking country to a de facto dual-language system in scarcely ten-fifteen years. Such changes which might take a hundred years to fully evolve (that is, in a country not taken by force) have happened so rapidly that many Americans are experiencing a sense of dislocation even disenfranchisement. We can send our sons and daughters halfway around the world to fight for the civil rights of people who may not even want us there but we can't secure our own damned borders from a foreign onslaught. And now there is evidence that the immigrants are not just coming from Mexico, they're coming also from Central and South America so how much longer will it be before we become just another banana republic like the ones the immigrants are fleeing from?

Quite apart from the whole immigration issue, if you want to see what a divided language does to a country, you need look no further than Canada where the English and the French have been battling for cultural and language supremacy for many years. Some years back, perhaps twenty, the French tried to secede formally from the English provinces. The difference is, their populations are already geographically segregated by their own volition; the United States' population is fully integrated. This is the stuff civil wars are made of.

So when, in the not too distant future, your grandkid can't get a job because he can't speak Spanish maybe then you'll understand, too late, just how much your country has changed.

Tony Hayward Redux

Tony Hayward is not an American. He is British. His company is not American. BP (British Petroleum) based in London, is a multi-national corporation as so many of today's big corporations are. But Hayward's statements and conduct during the worst oil spill in U.S. history, is very revealing about the differences in attitude between average citizens and the world's movers and shakers of business and government. Rarely has the arrogance of the privileged been on such gaudy and public display.

It started on April 20, 2010 when the Deepwater Horizon Well exploded in the Gulf of Mexico killing eleven workers on the oil rig and sending oil from a broken drill head gushing into the gulf for three punishing months. Chief Executive Hayward, seemingly unfazed by the spill, told reporters that he wished the disaster were over so he could "have my life back". In June while the oil continued to spill off the Louisiana coast, caused severe harm to wildlife, fishing and many cottage industries and lapped against American coastlines as far away as Florida, Hayward was spotted racing off the English Isle of Wight on his yacht "Bob" which he co-owned. His cavalier attitude toward the whole mess was not lost on the American public and he was subsequently replaced but the public relations damage had been done. BP's partners on the rig made charges of "gross negligence and/or willful misconduct". There were charges that BP cut corners on safety to speed up the drilling to save money and this will probably take years to sort out in the courts. But what is undisputable is that these high-flying thugs in business suits expect a free pass from any and all responsibility for their screw-ups and their frauds, no matter how egregious. We have seen this time and time again whether it's by the tobacco companies, polluting chemical companies, coal mine explosions, poisonous drugs and most recently, the banking industry fraud. And the real tragedy? Nine times out of ten, they get that free pass. You and I could go to jail for stealing a loaf of bread; they get to stroll away with their dignity and their millions (or billions) intact.

All men are created equal, but apparently, some men are created more equal than others.

Today's CEO's are paid obscene amounts of money to execute their one and only corporate mandate; to make as much profit as is humanly possible. The financial results of large, publicly-traded companies, which is the vast majority of them, are not judged each decade or even at the end of the year; they are judged every fiscal quarter with the expectation that each quarter will see a significant rise in earnings from the previous quarter. There is no other reason for corporations to exist, except to make a profit, no matter what kind of boloney their public relations departments try to feed you. They will and they do routinely sacrifice the health and safety of their employees in unsafe working conditions and you and your kids and your future offspring by dumping hazardous waste. They will and do mislabel and misrepresent their products and outright lie about their benefits. And congress? Let's just say they don't look too closely at even the most dangerous violations of the public welfare. Derivatives, anyone?

It is an understatement to say that the interests of corporate America are no longer the same as the interests of private-citizen America. In many ways, the goals of so-called American corporations vs. the welfare of average American citizens have veered off into totally opposite directions.

We used to have a saying back in the fifties," What's good for General Motors, is good for America" and in that prosperous, high-employment era the saying was literally true. GM's current struggle to be profitable in a very crowded global automotive marketplace, tells you just how much times have changed. With so many of our corporations now operating as multi-nationals, their profit interests are in many cases in direct conflict with the economic health, even the national security (see below) of the United States and its citizens. A tiny case in point; some people may be wondering at the decision by GM to dump the Pontiac brand, still a very popular car with many Americans. Well, it turns out that GM's new best friends, the Chinese, just love their Buicks. GM reasoned that it could not afford to keep both brands in manufacture. Looking at the potential market in China vs. the U.S. what would you do? Hey, it's not personal, it's just business. So why does our government continue to award tax breaks to these formerly all-American corporations for taking their facilities, their production, their jobs and their tax revenue overseas?

And the money! Holy mukluks, the compensation packages these guys take home make you want to cry. The average chief executive officer makes more money before lunch in one day, than his minimum-wage employee earns for the entire year. Notice I didn't say the CEO earns his money. With a pay ratio of approximately 821 to 1, how can we possibly say the boss "earns" his money? Steals is more accurate.

Perhaps a few specific examples will make the case. In the midst of large-scale lay-offs and home foreclosures approaching two million at this writing, America's top CEO's have weathered the recession handsomely. Annual salaries and bonuses in the millions of dollars a year were and are commonplace in mega-Corporateland such as: Ken Chenault, CEO, American Express, $6.33 Million; Ivan Seidenberg, CEO, Verizon, $5.5 Million; Ray Irani, CEO, Occidental Petroleum, $4.92 Million; David Novak, CEO, Yum Brands (Restaurants), $4.39 Million; Samuel Palmisano, CEO, IBM, 1.8 Million. Even these generous figures don't tell the whole compensation story. Among the top Fortune 500 companies, total compensation usually consists of not just salary and year-end bonuses, but also stock and stock options, accumulated pension balances and other deferred compensation which can easily add many more millions to the CEO's overall compensation package. So we find that although Ken

Chenault's salary and bonus in 2010 was $6.33 Million, his accumulated wealth balance with American Express was closer to $100 Million. Likewise, Ken Lewis, CEO of Bank of America who graciously took no salary during the recession nevertheless also had an accumulated wealth balance of over $100 Million with his employer, Bank of America. (Lewis retired at the end of 2009). Ray Irani, Occidental Petroleum, made $103 Million in 2010, largely because of $85 Million in "other" benefits. Even when the CEO's are walking away from their employers, they still manage to take a hefty part of the store with them. Fred Hassan, CEO of Schering-Plough presided over the merger between Schering and Merck and then took $49.6 Million with him when he left after the merger. The merger also cost 17,500 employees their jobs. The other three top officers of Schering received an additional $59 Million combined in golden parachutes for a grand total of $106 Million. Those 17,500 employees needn't wonder where their earnings went. They went directly into the pockets of Fred Hassan and the other three officers who engineered the merger. And speaking of lay-offs, the CEO's who take home the most money are also likely to have laid off the most employees: Verizon, 21,000 employees; American Express, 4,000 employees; Bank of America, 35,000 employees. It's a zero-sum game.

Since Barack Obama got stomped by the Republicans in the 2010 election, he's trying to make nice with the Republicans' sweethearts, Big Business. Toward that end, he has named Jeffrey Immelt, CEO of General Electric (GE) as Chairman of the Board of Outside Economic Advisers to the White House. Excuse me, but naming Immelt to advise our government about economic policy is like naming the fox to guard the hen house after the fox has eaten most of the chickens. GE derives 60% of its revenue and profit from foreign-based businesses. GE brags that although it paid no U.S. federal income tax in 2010, it has paid between $2 and 3 Billion a year in taxes to foreign countries where its factories reside and do business. This is all legal and thanks to the U.S. Tax Code, General Electric Company is able to deduct those foreign taxes it pays from its U.S. tax obligation. Questions: How exactly does this help the American worker when jobs representing 60% of GE's revenue have been exported to foreign countries? How does this scenario increase the U.S. tax revenue base? How does this help to decrease our country's ballooning budget deficits or our long term national debt (14.2 Trillion and climbing)? Oh, yes, a reminder: The Republicans in Congress think corporate taxes are too high.

In the recent great recession which we are still trying to dig our way out of, GE got burned by its participation in the sub-prime mortgage mess which reclassified it from a manufacturer to a financial services company and gutted its stock down to $16 a share on the New York Stock Exchange. GE is once again championing manufacturing but Americans will be aghast to learn that GE's latest manufacturing venture is an agreement with China to produce, in China, the avionics for China's new C919 commercial airliner. This agreement will result in the transfer of most of GE's advanced avionics technology in support of this joint venture. Of course, there is nothing to prevent the technology from being used in China's military aircraft. This type of technology transfer was strictly forbidden in the Washington in which I was employed not so many years ago. We have no military alliance with China. In fact, indications are that China sees itself as the next great military super-power. How can we be certain that China will always be our good buddies? They have already engineered/stolen a stealth aircraft. So get ready to eat their dust. Or their missiles.

As for Jeffrey Immelt, while he presided over the crash of GE's stock, his compensation package reached almost $100 Million Dollars in salary, bonuses, stock and stock options and accrued pension benefits.

So how much wealth is too much? How much bloated arrogance will the citizenry suffer? Remember Marie Antoinette? When told her subjects lacked bread to eat, she replied, "Then let them eat cake". Such are the stuff revolutions are made of and I suppose, Marie just lost her head.

Paybacks are a bitch. And we're going to get to them.

Businesses, Corporations And Profit 101

There are businesses and then there are corporations. When the country was young, early nineteenth century young, businesses and corporations were pretty much the same thing. Remember the nursery rhyme about the butcher, the baker, the candle-stick maker? Well, that's about all there was. Corporations existed but they were few and far between. Most businesses were very small, run by one person or one family. Beginning around 1815, after we defeated the British in another bruising war, we began in earnest the task of building home-grown American commerce. The South with its huge cotton crops turned to textiles. The Midwest became the country's breadbasket and the Northeast turned to manufacturing. Each section of the country complemented the others and the nation prospered. Corporations multiplied and also prospered. America went on to make immense achievements in technology and manufacturing. Henry Ford (1863-1947) is famous not only for the car that bears his name, but for the assembly-line manufacturing process he designed and implemented which greatly accelerated the production process. At the same time, Ford was smart enough to realize that it would do no good to build a million cars if no one could afford to buy them, so he established the first living wage for his workers.

We Americans invented the concept of mass production. It's in our DNA. First, we design a product on paper and then painstakingly, lovingly build the first one, the prototype, and refine it tirelessly until we can adapt it to large-scale manufacturing processes which can consist of some combination of automatic, machine-driven, human-interface component assembly. That's the most expensive part in the manufacturing cycle.

Once we turn on the manufacturing process and start large-scale production, we quickly recoup the research and development expense which went into building the prototype and begin to make a profit because mass-production is the profit-making end of the business. The more widgets we can produce and sell at a moderate price, the more profit we can make and the less it costs to make each unit, including the initial cost of research and development which is a dead loss. This is Economics 101. Everybody knows it. So why are American businesses willing, even anxious to off-shore the very processes which represent the money-making part of the cycle? We will answer that question shortly.

But moving on, in the service of this research, development and manufacturing cycle, we must hire people, lots of them, to implement all the various stages in bringing the new product to the market place. First of course, are the design engineers and draftsmen, followed by Production, Sales and Marketing, Accounting, Personnel, Quality Control, Shipping and Receiving and New Product R&D. Many outside services are also needed to assist our new manufacturing company starting with a real estate broker to locate a suitable facility to house production (most start-up companies are not wealthy enough to build their own facility), a printing company to produce the new letterhead and maybe an advertising company to tout the benefits of the new product. Employees also support the local economy in which the manufacturer is located by buying their lunch at the local luncheonette, opening an account at the local bank so they can cash their paychecks, shopping at local specialty stores for dry cleaning, hair cutting, greeting cards and on and on…

At each stage in the evolution of a product, more and more people are needed for the implementation, and more and more money changes hands. The more money that is earned, the more product can be bought. The more product which can be sold, the more product must be produced which can lead to expansion of the manufacturing facility or perhaps, the building of a brand new one (construction workers). And of course more employees must be hired to man the new facility. It's a closed circle where everybody produces, everybody earns, everybody spends, jobs increase, incomes surge, demand rises, manufacturing explodes. This is the essence of a healthy, dynamic capitalist system.

We have a 200-year economic culture of considering American Business as the life blood of American commerce, the chief engineer of job creation, wage production and the creation and nourishment of the middle class. For most of that 200 years, American businesses and corporations fulfilled that role completely. As previously noted, along about 1985, the U.S. significantly increased the off-shoring of routine manufacturing jobs to China. Even before that, Japan had been a major beneficiary of American largess but we still maintained vast manufacturing resources. Ronald Reagan changed all that with his anti-manufacturing economic policies and each president and congress since then has continued to tout the benefits of free trade even as whole industries have shut down in small towns across America and moved to foreign countries and jobs have disappeared forever. Americans who still have a job are seeing their wages continue to decline in real terms. Where we used to have an economy where Mom stayed home and raised the kids we now have an economy where Mom and Dad both work full-time and still can't make ends meet, that is if they are still able to find work.

While we continue to be a leader in scientific research and development, these efforts are mainly on-going at government-owned labs or government-funded universities. The fruits of these labors either die on the vine or are turned over to one of the big corporations which export any profitable manufacturing to a foreign country. In some cases our universities are collaborating with a foreign university from the git-go, agreeing to share any useful results of the research. Kumbayah.

And while the American worker continues to be squeezed by increasing population vs. decreasing job base, today's CEO's are not passing back the additional profits accruing to their companies as the result of using cheap foreign labor. Those excess profits are added to the bottom line of the corporations and the already exorbitant pay packages of the CEO's who have hijacked the jobs of Americans. And our government continues to reward these corporations for off-shoring our livelihoods with tax breaks and foreign-favored trade policies (although those foreign countries do not reciprocate) resulting in huge deficits which now threaten our very existence as a nation.

We have to give the Tea Party credit. At least, they had the guts to stand up and cry "Foul!" but let's hope they don't learn too late that they've thrown out the baby with the bath water.

Sorting Through All Those Goodies

Every time you purchase a product, look to see where it was made and remind yourself that that product, possibly carrying a U.S. logo, made by a manufacturer in China who then turned around and sold it back to the U.S. consumer, probably cost Americans hundreds, if not thousands, of U.S. jobs. Those American workers won't be supporting the American tax base, won't be contributing to the Social Security Trust Fund, won't be buying the products you make...Oops, I forgot. You don't make any products either. Your company's widgets are now made in Bangladesh. Or Mexico. Or Pakistan. Or India. Whatever country has the lowest wages, the least environmental protections, the smallest or no worker rights, even including child labor, that's the country that gets the license to manufacture the products we buy.

I promised early on that we wouldn't get into the boring minutia of numbers but I need to make an exception just this once. The American people need to see this. Following is our trade imbalance with China taken from the U.S. Government's own agency, the Census Bureau, starting with 1985, through 2010. Figures are in millions of dollars.

1985	-$6 million
1986	-$1,665 million
1987	-$2,796 million
1988	-$3,489 million
1989	-$6,234 million
1990	-$10,431 million

1991	-$12,691 million
1992	-$18,309 million
1993	-$22,777 million
1994	-$29,505 million
1995	-$33,789 million
1996	-$39,520 million
1997	-$49,695 million
1998	-$56,927 million
1999	-$68,677 million
2000	-$83,833 million
2001	-$83,096 million
2002	-$103,065 million
2003	-$124,068 million
2004	-$162,254 million
2005	-$202,278 million
2006	-$234,101 million
2007	-$258,506 million
2008	-$268,040 million
2009	-$226,877 million
2010	-$275,000 million

We export products to China of course, at the same time we import Chinese goods to the U.S. But notice the minus signs before each figure. These represent the net dollar loss -ours- after we subtract our exports to China. So in 2010, we imported $275 Billion more in goods then we exported to China. It does not help that as the Chinese economy has galloped ahead (their growth rate has been running between 9% and 12% a year) the Chinese have stubbornly kept their dollar (yuan) artificially low compared to the U.S. dollar and other currencies which has the effect of making the price of U.S. goods too high, even while making Chinese goods a comparative bargain.

Notice that in 2009 during the first year of the Obama presidency, our trade imbalance with China actually shrank. Of course it is still huge but at least it went in the right direction, down. It may be tempting for some folks to credit actions taken by the new Obama administration with the savings but in 2009 we were in the teeth of the worst economic crisis since the 1930's and business of all kinds came to a virtual stand-still. However, the slightly decreased trade imbalance does demonstrate "the power of the purse". In other words, if we want to rebuild our own economic base, we must decrease the number of products we buy from China and other foreign countries and increase the number of products we make here and buy here.

So as you sort through all your imported consumer toys, just once in awhile consider how much all those goodies are really costing us.

America, we're in a race to the bottom and nobody can change it but us.

The Big Squeeze

"If you can build a better mousetrap, the world will beat a path to your door."

Okay, so this old saying went out of style with the hula hoop. Today, we are more likely to be dealing with iPads than Edsels. But the sentiment hasn't changed. Through research, technical innovation, smart development and cost-effective manufacturing, global businesses strive to produce the products the world wants to buy. Even better if nobody else is making them. That's how fortunes are made.

And that's how America became the greatest economic power the world has ever known. At the end of World War II, all of Europe and part of Asia were ravaged by war and were in no position to turn out industrial or consumer goods. We became the candy store to the world. We made everything here, you name it: clothes, guns, cars, toasters, cookie-cutter homes, refrigerators, trains, baby shoes, light bulbs and aircraft engines; and we sold it all at a profit. From the mid-1940's through the 60's and into the 70's, we blew the doors off the economic world. We built on the legacy of Roosevelt's New Deal and when John Kennedy told us to fly to the moon, we did. Literally. And the prosperity was wide-spread; white collar, blue-collar, there were plenty of jobs to go around even with just a high school diploma. And incomes kept rising. This is not something I read about somewhere. I lived it. GE, Ford, GM, IBM, AT&T, for generations these names have been burned into the American psyche, we thought, forever. And even now, a job offer from one of these corporate giants is cause for a major celebration. It's really tough to even consider that these red, white and blue American fixtures are becoming less and less American and more and more foreign all the time and they're taking millions of formerly American jobs with them overseas, 5.5 million to 8.5 million jobs in the last ten years, depending on who's doing the counting.

So will we all find jobs eventually? Most of us will. Somehow. But with a steadily growing American and foreign population, chasing a steadily diminishing number of jobs, we can expect to command less and less of a take home pay (the Law of Supply and Demand). We may find the work to be intellectually challenging, exhausting even, but a job that might have paid $25/hour back in the go-go nineties may pay $12.50/hour today even though the cost of life's necessities, like food and shelter keep rising. And you will still be expected to be proficient on the computer and probably take on new and different responsibilities as more jobs are eliminated. If you don't like it, go work somewhere else. But where?

Will college graduates fare a lot better? Somewhat, but the depressing fact is that today's bachelor degree is fast becoming the equivalent of yesterday's high school diploma. Again, there simply are not enough jobs to go around. So quite a few students are now aiming for a master's degree or Ph.D. but even there, some fields are already experiencing a glut, most notably law.

It used to be in our manufacturing-rich economy that people of modest education, say a high school diploma and a year of college could gain on-the-job experience and work their way up to maybe Manager, Shipping Department or Supervisor, Production Department or Manager, Quality Control. The college grads became the vice presidents, CEO's and CFO's of these companies. And the wages were decent. Those jobs scarcely exist anymore. They were all exported along with a major portion of our product design and manufacturing expertise. It's tough to be a design engineer when there are fewer and fewer tangible products to design and engineer. Because we design and build less within our own borders we are losing the experience, the practical know-how, the understanding of how one system, or one component, or one substrate interacts with and affects others. Besides, engineering design jobs are among the easiest to export to a foreign country, thanks to the internet. So who needs an American engineer?

No job is safe. Just about any job that is, for the most part, knowledge-based can be exported. Very few jobs are indispensable unless you're a plumber, roofer, car mechanic or some other hands-on servicer. And yeah, you can also be a minimum wage stock clerk or cashier at Wal-mart. And don't think for a moment the politicians don't realize what an impossible situation they've put us in. They do. They don't care. Because the average American making somewhere south of $100,000 a year does not pay for their reelection campaigns.

And what of today's many millions of citizens who have no college background? What happens to them? Not everyone is destined for higher education. Many people simply don't have the mental aptitude to make it through college. Many come from really sketchy family backgrounds and may lack the basic understanding of how to function in a high-tech, educated society. They may not even have a high school diploma. These are also Americans. In an increasingly complex economy with continually decreasing manufacturing jobs, these Americans are considered to be throw-aways. No wonder we have a vast coast-to-coast sub-economy of drug-pushing and prostitution. When there is no dignity or self-respect left, people still have to survive.

Tea And Nihilism

We Americans are economically stretched to the breaking point and shaken in our core belief that every generation would be able to achieve even greater success than our parents. Road rage, angry outbursts in public places, school children bullying classmates, domestic violence, school and workplace massacres, all are symptomatic of a citizenry feeling out of control and striking out at whomever is closest, each other. And while we try desperately to restore some order to our lives, we can't get at the economic royalists who are really responsible for our country's economic decline. These titans of banking, industry and government, many of whom should be in jail, are safely locked inside their gated, security alarmed, dog- protected communities and don't have to deal with society's rabble, i.e. us. So we are very angry and this free-floating rage toward everything and everyone has spawned a new and vocal addition to the political scene, the Tea Party.

The Teabaggers advocate for smaller government and lower taxes. Beyond that, they seem to believe they are just trying to reestablish the values and religious beliefs of old (because Glenn Beck said so). What the teabaggers don't realize or understand, is that they are moving away from the traditional concepts of democracy and toward nihilism. They are dismissing the unity of one nation indivisible, discounting the mutual benefits and responsibilities of community and citizenship, rejecting the moral high ground of charity, compassion and contributing their fair share to the kitty. Yes, they want all the benefits, social security, medicare, pensions, capital gains, etc., they just don't want any of the responsibility of being part of the larger American community which includes helping the poor, the old and infirm, the mentally and physically handicapped, the uninsured, which are also part of America. They want to down-size government, sure. But as soon as something goes wrong, they are the first to cry "Where is the government? Why don't they do something?" Moreover, the Tea Party doesn't seem to have any comprehensive goals for our nation's future, any plan, any priorities to unite them. Polls taken by the New York Times and just about everybody else have failed to identify a single specific program that the Tea Party would be willing to reduce funding for, much less eliminate except foreign aid, a total of 1% of the federal budget. So the Teabaggers want what they want when they want it. And what is that exactly? Nobody knows, least of all the Tea Party.

Instead of doing some tedious homework about the long term and continuing causes of our country's problems, the Teabaggers would rather fly across the country to meet their like numbers for a spirited exchange of ignorances. They vent their anger and grievances and all-around gimmies to a sympathetic audience then jet home secure in their self-righteous rage. And as we know, greed sells. Ask the Republicans. They are the creators of the something-for-nothing mantra, the purveyors of the free-lunch philosophy. The Republicans, with an able assist from the Democrats, are also the party which has done the most to impoverish average Americans by presiding over and encouraging with the U.S. tax code, the wholesale export of American industries and American jobs. But don't try to tell that to the Tea Party. They are way too invested in bashing anyone who suggests that maybe the issues are a little more complicated than smaller government equals smaller taxes equals prosperity forever.

And it's not just the money. There is a heavy price to be paid for all this anger and divisiveness. Instead of a coast-to-coast community of patriotic Americans united in our profound resolve as we experienced for a brief moment after 9/11, we have regressed back to a very primitive tribe mentality where us-against-them is a constant back-drop to our lives. We regard any stranger with a jaundiced eye, waiting to see what his game is.

Gone is the fellowship of shared deprivation of the WWII era when we felt we were all in this together, we Americans fighting against a well-known evil. Today, it's every tribe, every man, for himself.

So, there's the White Tribe, the Black Tribe, the recently emerged Latino Tribe (just what we need, another divisive tribe), a multitude of religious tribes, and of course, the Democratic, Republican and Tea Bag tribes. We can't get at the sonofabitches who are really causing us so much pain so we turn on each other, like a pack of dogs fighting for that last bone. We come together not as friends, not as a community, but as strategic allies, temporarily, to defeat the agenda of one or the other tribes and then we disband and retreat back to the safety of our home caves until we feel the survival imperative to ritualistically attack one of the other tribes again.

It's working. Sort of. But we may have noticed that we feel increasingly isolated and dislocated from our fellow Americans, believing we have nothing in common and the glue of community and sharing is becoming weaker and weaker threatening to simply collapse. The blind, relentless profiteering, the gotcha news media, the cynical lying politicians, the unequal application of the law and society's norms, the smug and hypocritical religious establishment, the greed and selfishness expressed throughout all of our institutions, our "tribes" if you will, all are signs that our society is breaking down and may not have much more time to run.

Look around you. Where do you think we're headed? What do you think is our country's future?

There Is No Such Thing As A Free Lunch

In the last twenty-five years, the economic policies of the last four presidents have totally reversed the mighty engine of the New Deal, brought the American worker to his knees, and destroyed the economic rationale of one of our most effective modern presidents, F.D.R., all the while lying to the American people that free trade with other countries would create more jobs for Americans.

Nothing in life is free. Everything costs something. Everything involves trade-offs. If I buy that new car now, it will deplete my college fund. If I take that new job paying more money, I'll have to sell the house and move across country. If we have kids right now my husband or I will have to quit work to care for them. I need to ask for a raise but I'm not even sure how secure my job is…

There is no such thing as a free lunch. There never was. There never will be.

If we continue to demand cheap imported products, we must deal with the fact that we are destroying our own labor base that pays the bills. If we want to be only an information technology country instead of a manufacturer, we have to be prepared to speak with customer service reps in India and other foreign countries since IT support jobs are the very easiest employment to export. If we want a 5% across-the-board tax cut which will put $1500 into the pocket of the average $30,000/year worker, we must also agree to the same 5% tax cut for the millionaire which is worth $50,000 in his pocket and at this juncture in history since we are actually broke, any tax cuts will have to be paid for by borrowing money, probably from China. How's that for mortgaging our children's future? If we want to be compassionate to the plight of illegal aliens and their children, we must accept that it will be at the expense of our own children. If we insist on starting another war every few years and have to fix up the damage we cause, as well as bribing the locals for their grudging support, we will have to continue to live with our own crumbling infrastructure for many more years into the future while spilling the blood of our sons and daughters all across foreign lands.

There is no such thing as a free lunch. Think about that the next time you go to the polls to vote. Is this or that politician making a realistic case in what he/she promises you? What is she actually doing, not just saying? Is he saying anything of value at all or are his pronouncements just telling us what we want to hear so we can comfortably duck any responsibility as citizens? In the 2010 elections, the winning slogan was smaller government, lower taxes, more jobs, and two and two equals five. And that's what most Americans voted for. Get ready to be disappointed again because...

there is no such thing as a free lunch.

Parsing The Vote

Votes have consequences. Long term, far-reaching consequences. Each president leaves a long-lasting, if not permanent mark on the country which will reverberate down through the decades ultimately affecting our lives in very personal ways, for good or for ill. While Franklin Roosevelt gave us the social security system, Ronald Reagan gave us a wildly lopsided tax system which accrued benefits to the rich at the expense of the middle class and also launched the beginning of the end of our industrial supremacy, Bill Clinton gave us NAFTA and the repeal of the Glass-Steagall Act and George Bush gave us the Iraq war, twelve million illegal aliens and more tax cuts for the rich.

Barack Obama was in the White House scarcely two years before the pundits starting calling for his head. Two whole years and he was unable to reverse the decline of an economy that has been committing slow-motion fiscal suicide for decades. No one seemed to understand the fact, certainly no one mentioned, that Obama was not in the White House alone. He shared the Oval Office with the policies of at least the last four presidents and the laws passed, or repealed, by their respective congresses. It has taken fully twenty-five years to bring the country to the edge of the cliff and very, very few Americans realize just how close we came to going over it in 2008. When a new president takes office we seem to think the clock starts over. Just like watching a thirty-minute sitcom, at the end of the thirty minutes, we wipe the slate clean and go on to the next show. Everything starts over from the beginning; new show, new president, it's all the same. Right?

But in truth, when new presidents set the agendas for their administrations, they are limited by the policies followed by their predecessors. They are further limited by a hostile, uncooperative congress. Then we, the voter, compound the presidents' limitations when we vote to change the political parties majorities in congress every couple of years before we've given the new president's policies a chance to work. Not surprisingly, when we change the balance of power in congress, the new majority will spend the next two years, not in trying to move the country forward, but in trying to reverse whatever progress was accomplished in the last two years. Consider the statement made by Mitch McConnell shortly before becoming the new Majority Leader in the Senate. He said that his top priority would be to "defeat Barack Obama in 2012". This, while 15 million Americans were out of work. We say we want congress to work together to get things done then we vote in a way that guarantees gridlock and vitriol. What are we missing?

In the 2010 election cycle, some voters said they voted against the incumbents to "send a message". But who did they really hurt more than themselves? We vote to send these men and women to Washington to represent us, the People. If all we're going to do is vote our spite, our anger, our bitterness, we might as well just stay home because we're wasting our vote. Likewise, when we vote for Democrats or Republicans solely because our family has always voted that way, we're not taking into account that parties change, philosophies change, circumstances change, and we are again wasting our vote.

We have at our disposal the most precious gift, still denied to much of the rest of the world; free, coast-to-coast and very public elections. You would think that we would honor this privilege by diligently researching each candidate, comparing notes with our family, friends and neighbors, asking tough questions and asking again when the answers are not forthcoming. Instead, we latch on to the first television sound-bite that sounds plausible like "take back America" or "change we can believe in" or we gobble up the hatred-filled candidate attacks and scandals, race baiting and misogyny and march into the voting booth full of righteous indignation, primed to give that voting machine a piece of our mind.

There are reasons why things happen as they do; solid, objective, grounded in reality reasons why one guy gets elected and another guy doesn't. And that reason is the number of votes cast. The electoral college does figure into it however, the electoral college seldom prevails against a popular groundswell, as Barack Obama demonstrated in 2007. When we casually cast a vote for one candidate or the other, especially for president, we seldom reflect that we will have plenty of time to regret our choice in leisure but that is exactly what happens.

If we were to advertise to hire a data entry clerk, we would ask our applicants if they could type. If we go out to hire a pharmacist we would want to know if the applicants understand chemistry, human biology and other drug-related subjects and that they have the degrees to support their experience. When there is money involved, we can be just as hard-nosed as the best of them. Why then do we vote for our officials because we "like" them? I remember that when George W. Bush was running for president the most common opinion voiced about him was that he was a regular guy, a nice guy, someone you'd like to have a beer with. No one, including members of his own party, spoke of his superior intellect, his experience in foreign affairs or his keen understanding of economics. After several months of legal wrangling because of perhaps the closest presidential vote in history, Bush claimed the presidency in 2000 and over the next eight years demonstrated what you get when you elect your drinking buddy to the White House.

If Al Gore had been sworn in as president in 2001 instead of George W. Bush we almost certainly would not have invaded Iraq and 4,400 citizen-soldiers would probably still be enjoying their kids today. Many more thousands would still have all their limbs, their eye sight and other senses and many more would be able to sleep a dreamless sleep. If Al Gore can be taken at his word, we would have been much further along on environmental issues, including our own alternative energy manufacturing base, social security funds would be in a lock box, and yes, we probably would have pursued Osama bin Laden into Afghanistan after 9/11, and stayed until we finished the job, not waited til 2009 to increase our forces there, long after we had lost all the momentum and sympathetic support of our allies.

Nothing exists in a vacuum. Everything we do in life affects something else. And again, votes have consequences, long-term, far-reaching, often irreversible, consequences. Just ask the parents of the soldiers who came home in body bags from Iraq, and ask the families of the young people who came home in broken pieces or with minds forever tortured by the carnage of war.

It's My Party And I'll Lie If I Want To

As stated previously, politicians lie. As far as which political party lies the most, I'm not sure it really matters. What does matter is that our entrenched, two-party system has become a sinister and dangerous force in our country whose members serve only to perpetuate themselves and their Greed-R-Us corporate patrons, while increasingly and alarmingly undermining the rights of the American people. I do not make this charge lightly. As a decades-long student of American governance and politics and the U.S. Constitution, I state with conviction that either we change the way in which we are governed or surely a popular uprising will change it for us, destroying the greatest hope for all mankind the world has ever known.

Corporations are not the people. The Constitution was written to establish a republic for the people. The Bill of Rights was added to protect the rights and liberties of the people. Nowhere in the Constitution does it talk about the rights and liberties of corporations except for a vague reference to "regulate commerce…" (Article I, Section 8). Nowhere in our Constitution is the right given to corporations to pollute our air and water, to seize property to build a private golf course, to extort money from the people by arbitrarily raising interest rates on loans, to sell dangerous drugs (including tobacco) while knowing of the risks, to sacrifice the safety of workers in mines and on oil rigs to maximize profits. Why did I write this book? I've asked myself that question many times. And I think it's because I reached a point in my life where I could not, not write the book.

If corporations are not the people, politicians are not the government. Again, our government derives its authority from the Declaration of Independence, the Constitution of the United States and the Amendments, and the Bill of Rights (the first ten amendments to the Constitution). I'm repeating myself. I know. The politicians, always looking for an angle to exploit, have recently found it fashionable to talk about "getting back to constitutional government". It makes a good slogan. But these guys know full well that probably only one American in a hundred has a clue what that means and that one-in-a-hundred American understands enough about the Constitution to know that Bush and Cheney should have been impeached by congress in 2003. But we digress.

From our country's very earliest beginnings, politics, like diplomacy, has always been about the art of the possible, the grand compromise. Our very own Ben Franklin, master craftsman of scientific invention and astute diplomat and politician was able to secure a political and military alliance with France which was to prove vital to the survival of our fledgling country. We didn't even have political parties back then and our nation did just fine.

Now, watching the partisan spectacle taking place in the U.S. Congress is like watching a food fight in the school cafeteria. Every day. In front of the whole country and the world. It's embarrassing and degrading to our country. Moreover, when our elected officials care far more about furthering the power of their political parties then they care about serving the country, we no longer have representative government; we just have a new version of totalitarianism with mindless profiteering as the all-consuming dictator.

There is an alternative which is gradually working its way into the American psyche. Already we are being told that the independent voter is the fastest growing segment of the electorate. Two of our elected U.S. senators are self-proclaimed independents. In the 2010 election cycle, many candidates ran as independents. At least one candidate won as a write-in candidate.

Clearly, this is a trend in the making although slowly. There is nothing wrong with individual citizens voting independently, however, without the structure of a political party the unaffiliated voter has no organizational clout, lacks the ability to change the status quo and so, just goes back and forth, voting for the Democrats one year, the Republicans the next. Net forward progress: zero.

But suppose we had not two major political parties, but three? The third party (let's call them the Moderates Party) could draw support from both the Republican and Democratic parties, effectively reducing each party's numerical power by as much as one third. No more splitting hairs or 50-50 votes. The beauty of having a third political party in our constitutional system is that the third party could vote with either the Democrats or the Republicans on every single program to come before the congress, ensuring true majority rule. Also, independent legislators could propose their own legislative agenda, making it virtually impossible for an us-against-them mentality to prevail. It would totally shake up the balance of power in congress. The corporate lobbyists would go nuts. They wouldn't be able to figure out who to buy off.

This concept of party coalitions is not new. It is practiced with some variation in a large number of countries, Germany, Israel and Italy to name a few. Most startling, Great Britain has for the first time in peacetime history, elected a coalition government in 2010 comprised of the Liberal Democrat's Nick Clegg as Deputy Prime Minister and the Conservative's David Cameron as Prime Minister. The Labor Party's Gordon Brown was defeated but presumably there are still Labor Party influences in play. The coalition concept ensures that no one party can amass unique power, nor any two parties create the kind of deadlock we have experienced in recent years.

So should we call for a constitutional amendment to create a third political party? Totally unnecessary. There is nothing in the U.S. Constitution that addresses politics, only governance. And yet, our two-party system is literally tearing the country apart from within. It is time for the American people to consign the two-party system to the trash heap of history where it belongs before our nation is damaged beyond repair. Again the politicians are not the government. We, empowered by our Constitution, are the People who must consent to be governed and it's time we remind the politicians of that fact.

So how can we capitalize on this growing block of disaffected voters? Start where all great American endeavors start, at the grass roots. Encourage local, state and even national candidates to run as independents. Contrary to popular belief it is not always necessary to run with a major political party to be a candidate for office. In most states a number of signatures must be obtained but this is usually a manageable number. Make the medium the message. The candidates should run openly on a platform of creating a third, more moderate power in American politics. Other than that one requirement the candidates message should be as broad-based as possible, neither left nor right, and should espouse the same basic tenets as the other major parties, without the cultural and religious grandstanding; governance by the U.S. Constitution, a strong military defense, clean air and water, education of our children, etc. Once the public grasps the advantages of electing independent candidates, momentum will take over. What starts rather spontaneously will eventually coalesce into a more formal structure. And while it is true that a number of alternative parties already exist; the Green Party, Libertarian Party, etc. these parties are either too narrowly focused or too extreme. To some, the Tea Party movement smacks of anarchy (little or no taxation, small, ineffectual government). No, this really is the time for middle-of-the-road candidates.

Who will support these candidates? Where will the money come from? The same place all the other candidates get it; from the American people. Don't forget the internet. Never before have we had such a powerful tool to appeal to every citizen to help change the direction of the country.

So in naming this budding new political party why not go with the name that is already on the lips of many a pundit; the Independents' Party? After all, that's how the whole thing got started a few years back, in a war for independence. Kind of fitting don't you think?

Et Tu Brute?

So far we've only skewered two branches of our government, the executive (the president) and the legislative (congress). That leaves the judiciary.

The U.S. Constitution provides for one Supreme Court and "such inferior courts as the Congress may...establish". Appointments to the supreme court are for life and they "shall hold their offices during good behaviour". Cases pled before the Supreme Court have typically first been heard in lower courts and then appealed upward. The Supreme Court picks and chooses which cases it wants to try. It is a voluntary decision. There are many more cases appealed to the Supreme Court then the court can actually try. The Supreme Court is the court of last resort in interpreting the Constitution with respect to case law.

For at least a hundred years, the court has upheld federal restrictions on the role corporations may play in elections. It was understood that the Constitution was written by the people, for the people, human people, not pieces of paper. And give credit where credit is due, our government has done a pretty good job of protecting the right of free speech guaranteed to the people since 1791 by the First Amendment to the Constitution. Until now.

With the U.S. Supreme Court's decision in January 2010 that corporations can give unlimited amounts of money to elect political candidates and they do not have to identify where the money is coming from, we have reached a critical new level in dangerous American governance.

It is one thing for the states to grant a charter to a group of citizens called a "corporation" to act as one unit in legal affairs. This legal charter enables the group, the corporation, to sell stock, to buy and sell real estate, to set up factories and offices, to hire and fire employees, to produce products and services, to sell to the public and to seek legal remedies in disputes. Corporate law is, as it should be, a totally separate practice from laws governing individuals (people, human). It is quite another thing to try to super-impose the privileges of real personhood on a system that has more in common with robots than it does with human beings. Corporations exist for one reason and one reason only: to make a profit. On a scale of one to ten, making a profit occupies all ten priorities. Human attributes didn't make the list.

There is nothing, absolutely nothing, in the U.S. Constitution that even hints at the proposition that a corporation should enjoy the same rights and privileges as a human American citizen. There is a rather vague reference to regulating commerce. That is all. A general corporation is a paper construct where responsibility is dispersed among a wide number of people. The bigger the corporation, the more diluted the individual's accountability and responsibility is. So is blame. If an individual breaks the law, he can be jailed. It is not possible to "jail" a corporation and since so many people are operationally involved in the corporation it is virtually impossible to assign responsibility and blame for anything to any one specific person. The burden of proof is just too high. This fact goes a long way toward explaining why a private citizen has little or no chance in protecting himself from the wrong-doing of a corporation or in successfully suing a corporation once he is harmed. There is an inherent conflict of interest between the private citizen and the corporation which we are discussing in this book. And in a legal contest you, very probably, lose.

Many Americans are increasingly alarmed by what they see as growing intrusion by the federal government into their private lives. They are so alarmed in fact that they fail to recognize the larger, more immediate, more insidious danger coming from the Big Business profit motive which drives just about everything in daily American life, far more than the government could hope to, at least, in the near term.

Look around. From the moment our feet hit the floor in the morning til we lay our weary heads back on our pillows, we are assaulted by messages about spending our money. The ads scream at us all the time, from everywhere: buy, gain, invest, save, get yours, order now, borrow, pay less, listen! Important! Urgent! Every aspect of our lives, our culture, our priorities, our education, our morals, our houses of worship, our social lives, are all orchestrated by the imperative of big businesses to make ever larger profits at our expense. Even our kids become unwitting hucksters of whatever junk business is pushing, be it candied cereal, sexy toy dolls or the latest violent, sadomasochistic video game. Get to the kids while they're young and oh, so malleable. That's the key. And those kids will sail right through life with a mouthful of gimmes and pass on the same consumerism values to their kids. Slowly, almost imperceptibly we are being enslaved to the primary directive to be enthusiastic little consumers, while we make the rich, richer. So we get to brag to our neighbors and co-workers about our new toys. Is this quality of life? Is it really worth it?

It is to this ruthless, amoral, profit-obsessed gang of corporate miscreants that the Supreme Court has bestowed all the benefits and privileges of the title of "person".

What does this have to do with jobs? Just this: Political advertising by corporations and not-for-profit PAC's, such as the U.S. Chamber of Commerce (not to be confused with the federal Department of Commerce) has the effect of confusing the issues and further dividing the electorate, based not on facts but on lies and scare tactics, exactly the same kind of manipulation the politicians use now to create phony issues and drive unyielding wedges between us and frighten our seniors with bizarre predictions (remember death panels?). And people, especially uninformed people, vote their fears. In the end we wind up electing the very politicians who happily throw the American worker under the bus, in order to appease the corporations that keep them in office, those same corporations which have already cost the U.S. millions of manufacturing jobs. I mentioned the U.S. Chamber of Commerce which is a very thinly-disguised Republican PAC (Political Action Committee). It has been widely reported that this 501.c non-profit spent $75 million in the 2010 election cycle to elect Republican candidates to congress and state governorships. Many of the TV ads they sponsored made negative, misleading assertions about the Democratic candidates. As we know, the Republicans swept the board in 2010 and we are now living with the results. That's what it has to do with jobs.

The Republican congress, the corporations and their lobbyists tell us that raising taxes on businesses and rich investors sends jobs overseas. Truthfully, that ship has sailed, years ago. And the companies which remain in this country do so not out of patriotism but out of the economy of staying geographically close to their customer, the American consumer.

Finally, the recent Supreme Court decision giving corporations the benefits of a "person" and the unfettered right to advertise and campaign for political candidates is not only a dangerous usurpation of the rights of American citizens, but it is, frankly, unconstitutional. It is only a matter of time until corporations are granted the right to vote just like we citizens do. That is the next logical step in an illogical progression.

And then at some point, the Court may decide that since corporations are so invested in American governmental affairs because of their sheer financial size, there is no need for American citizens to vote at all. Besides, we show so little interest in voting now. So why not give the vote to the crooks? We already have the foxes (congress) guarding the hen house.

And yet, they still keep telling us that we are free citizens. Are we? And if so, for how much longer?

Where Is Our Moon Shot?

The date was July 20, 1969. All over America children were being excused from classrooms so they could watch the landing of Apollo 11 on the moon. Me too. My college accounting class gathered in front of an old TV, lent for the occasion and we all watched in rapt silence as Astronaut Neil Armstrong announced "The Eagle has landed". Soon he descended down the ladder to the moon's surface and said, "That's one small step for man, one giant leap for mankind" and so it was. America made global history on that day and fulfilled the goal set by President John F. Kennedy in 1961, although Kennedy did not live to see the incredible event. Just think of it. In eight short years, we came from behind Communist Russia's first man to achieve sub-orbital flight to the history-making moon landing.

The Kennedy years were tragically brief, less than a full term. Yet his legacy reverberates still today. Kennedy shares a lot of the admiration and devotion accorded to Franklin Roosevelt before him. And like Roosevelt, Kennedy gave us so much more than a program to invest in. He gave us inspiration. He gave us a big goal and told us how to get there. He rekindled our energy and focused our nation's drive. He gave us hope and then delivered on his promise. And we were so very proud of our country.

Can you imagine the U.S. achieving such a monumental feat today? With the very tall five-year old delinquents we have running our congress? A big item for which the Republican Party is justly criticized is their continuous nay-saying. No matter what President Obama proposes in order to achieve a positive economic momentum, the Republicans shoot it down. You won't hear them propose any job-creating initiatives of their own. They are content to attack the oppositions' plans as bad, can not work, benefit's the wrong people, costs too much, hurts business, etc. We used to call this a defeatist attitude. The Republicans just call it conservatism. Maybe it's the same thing. One thing is for sure; if you believe you can't achieve something, you are right. Small wonder the Republicans are called the party of "no".

There is a residual side-effect to all this nay-saying. If success breeds success, it is also true that pessimism breeds failure. And there is a pall of failure and hopelessness hanging over America today that some of us older folks have not seen before in our lifetime. And the Republicans don't offer any positive ideas to push the country forward. Their strategy is to be as vague as possible in order to present the smallest target possible. Of course, they're always in favor of more tax cuts for the rich.

It's the Democrats' fault too. They have gone way too far with this bleeding-heart welfare state. Everyone has an outlandish sense of entitlement; everybody has their hand out, no one more so than the big corporations. The Democrats taught them how to do it.

So here we are in the twenty-first century, our hopes and dreams badly battered if not shattered altogether. Nobody seems to have any real answers. The politicians, depending on which party, advocate for small government/big government, deficit spending/deficit reduction, tax cuts/tax increases, spend/save, stimulate the economy/pay down the debt. It isn't who's right and who's wrong. The fact is, they're focusing on the wrong issues. Kennedy and Roosevelt were both visionaries. Neither one of them focused on garroting the buck. What they did do is envision the exciting potential of our nation, set the challenging goals to motivate us and then execute those programs which would turn their visions into real achievement. Balanced budgets and a thriving economy are the result of the successful achievement of a country's ambitious goals, not of counting Scrooge's money bags.

Good God, how our dreams, our goals have been emasculated!

We have come from the lofty achievement of putting a man on the moon, to the anguished wrangling over what to do with 14 million unemployed. I lay this squarely at the doorstep of the greed of both the mega-corporations and the politicians who go out of their way to protect them, resulting in the mass exodus of our manufacturing base and the near collapse of our once thriving economy.

About the only remedy the Republicans and the Tea Party have offered is cutting government spending to reduce the deficit, a noble goal to be sure. The problem is, we can not deficit-reduce our way back to prosperity. That is not how wealth is made. Wealth is created by adding value to raw resources, turning them into useful, saleable products and educating young people so they can perform valuable services, like computer programming. This is the stuff the world is willing to pay for. This is how wealth is created. Unfortunately, when those useful products are made in China and the computer programming is done in India, while it enriches the corporations, it doesn't do a damned thing for the American workforce or our U.S. tax base.

So what is our moon shot? Bring back manufacturing. We never should have allowed it to leave our shores. But let's do it in a whole new way. How? Read on.

A New Kid On The Block

Nothing spurs competition quite like the new kid on the block, particularly if that new kid has toys we want but don't have. So let's create a new, alternative capitalism to compete with the old capitalism. If our old traditional corporations don't want to hire and don't want to invest in America, the hell with them. Let 'em keep the $1.8 Trillion Dollars they are reportedly hoarding. And good riddance to them! We will go around them. Go over them. Go under them. But we will create American jobs for the American people.

Create a new federal department called "the Department of Domestic Research, Development and Manufacturing (DRDM). Business participation would be strictly voluntary. Companies that want a piece of the pie (funding, access) would have to agree to keep all their operations, including jobs, inside the U.S. Foreign companies could also play as long as they agree to build their factories here and hire our domestic workforce. Violations would result in the loss of their funding and stiff penalties on top of that. Since most of our mega-buck American corporations are already multi-national enterprises, there would be little or no competition coming from that quarter (but plenty of protest!). Maybe they could spin off new small companies (wholly independent) to get a piece of the action.

Under this brand new U.S. job-creating department we can include the following:

- The Small Business Administration. Give it more clout and more funding.

- A new public relations bureau to explain, educate and sell the overall mission of DRDM to the American people. For the most part, we will find a very receptive audience. The exception of course will be big business and their hangers-on politicians. A way around them would be for the President to sell the concept directly to the American people and once the interest is established, he could then dare the Republicans to shoot it down.

- Create a new agency within the DRDM Department to fund promising research and development (R&D) leading to manufacturing. Any small company with a serious technical proposal could submit it to this agency for review and potential funding. A similar agency already exists. DARPA is the preeminent federal agency responsible for the funding of development of new technologies. Recently, it had an annual budget of $3B. Many of the most productive and ambitious ideas for technical innovation originated within the DARPA framework. The DARPA organizational model is, itself, sophisticated, timely and radical by the standards of traditional hierarchies and could probably only flourish in a non-profit environment. Yet, the spin-offs from the DARPA teams have resulted in truly history-making breakthroughs (the internet was one of them) which probably would have been unattainable any other way. So elegantly purpose-driven is the DARPA organizational model that I have included it in the appendix to this book. There's just one little problem to all this wonderfulness: DARPA is an acronym for the "Defense Advanced Research Projects Agency", DARPA's boss is the Department of Defense and DARPA's mission is to develop military technologies. There is no one equivalent federal agency to guide R&D efforts in the private or "civilian" sector. That's supposed to fall within the purview of for-profit businesses in our capitalist system and it's a privilege that is protected by the federal government. More and more however, American corporations are not only derelict in their funding of R&D, but AWOL altogether; hence, the need for a civilian version of DARPA. "CARPA" springs to mind.

- Next, we must add an agency to locate, interview and award full scholarships to individuals with innovative ideas which could lead to tangible products and services. We squander far too much superior brain power in this country even while the U.S. is falling far behind the rest of the world in math, science and other technical academic achievements. We need to develop a way to find people with the intellect and the drive to create, but perhaps lacking the funds, harness their potential and give them the tools to translate good ideas into profitable products. This is not about giving someone a free ride. It's about making the most of our natural resources. I contend our immigration policies should reflect our need to grow our scientific capital. Keep in mind, we're not talking about the mass production of whoopee cushions; we're talking about "building better mousetraps", practical, producible ideas that have a recognizable utility. Many such technologies are being developed right now. And as we shall learn in the next chapter, they're coming from some unusual places.

- The Department of Domestic Research, Development and Manufacturing should create its own X-Prize. An explanation is in order. The X Prize Foundation is a non-profit organization which designs and manages public competitions intended to encourage technological development which could benefit mankind. The first X Prize was awarded to Charles Lindbergh for his 1927 nonstop flight between New York and Paris. In 2004, the Ansari X Prize was awarded to the first privately financed team that could build and fly a three-passenger vehicle into sub-orbital space twice within two weeks Twenty-six teams participated in that one and spent more than $100 million to win the $10 million prize. It was won by Mojave Aerospace Ventures. Numerous other private X prizes have since spun off. Our new Department of DRDM could sponsor the American X Prize. Here are just a few of the challenges which the American X-Prize could address:

One of the first projects I would fund would be the creation of an additional, super-secure, closed-end internet to protect our infrastructure, such as our power grid, banking systems and military operations from hackers with sinister intent.

Then there's also:

- Design a way to safely dispose of and/or deactivate nuclear waste.
- Design a cheap way to desalinate sea water.
- Design, deploy a universal relational data base to identify no-fly terrorists.
- Design a cheap, portable way to make polluted water potable.
- Cold fusion, anyone?
- Design, deploy cheap, portable charging stations for electric vehicles. (This may already be covered).
- Design a way to equalize flood vs. drought, from coast to coast (national underground piping system?)
- Design a strong, collapsible carrier to move drinking water to areas ravaged by hurricanes, etc. (Perhaps the carriers could be transported under helicopters and dropped without landing.)

For the longer term, we must accept that our traditional manufacturing sponsors have changed the game plan and the change is permanent; therefore, we must make new allies, create new synergies and form new partnerships to move our country forward. Read on.

Schools Of Learning;
Universities Of Making Stuff

The U.S. has a capitalist economic structure. Fair enough. Show me where it is written in our Constitution that we can not have multiple capitalist systems in our society, sometimes collaborating but at other times, competing against each other. Where do the best and the brightest research minds hang their hats? The corporate sector? Some. But many also choose the kinder, gentler atmosphere of government-funded laboratories and private/public universities. These people are most likely drawn to research and development because they truly enjoy the work, not because they're chasing a buck. We have pretty much ignored this national treasure for too long. It is time to bring it into the forefront of our economic landscape and give it a continuous and long-term mission: Putting Americans back to work.

Some critics will tell you that unlike funding of the military, the federal government has no constitutional mandate to participate in non-defense job creation. To which I reply, it does if the country's national security is threatened and I can think of no more dangerous long-term threat to our national security than millions of angry, restless, unemployed and underemployed young people. Further, when Roosevelt created the CCC and the PWA to put starving Americans to work, was that considered unconstitutional? When Kennedy vowed to put a man on the moon and then marshaled the resources to accomplish it, did anyone complain that was unconstitutional? We have a long and well-established precedent for federal involvement in the economic development of our citizenry. We can and we must turn our attention to this vital mission once again. The alternative is unthinkable.

It's a matter of emphasis and scale, really. The federal government currently funnels massive amounts of money to the private sector, buying everything from tanks to toothbrushes from corporations large and small, domestic and foreign. Meanwhile we give pittance in grants to our schools of higher learning, even though it is the universities and labs, some of them federally-owned, which are producing the most exciting and promising research. Our major corporations pretty much abandoned R&D decades ago. If they can't produce a profitable product in a couple of fiscal quarters, they just aren't interested. It is precisely this short-term thinking that has resulted in our historic decline among our peers, first Japan and now China. So why not start adjusting our funding priorities to favor the institutions which are doing the most to insure America's growth and future prosperity?

One of the very first things we need to do is create college-level courses and a degree in Manufacturing Technology. No, I'm not talking about the degrees in business administration which already exist in every major college in the country. Recently in a TV interview it was revealed that existing manufacturers are complaining that they can't hire laid-off workers because they "don't have the right skill sets to run the sophisticated equipment". CAD-CAM (computer-aided design and computer-aided manufacturing has been with us now for over 25 years, becoming more and more sophisticated as the years go by, but most of the beneficiaries of this know-how have been foreign countries because so much of our manufacturing base has been off-shored to them. The fact that we have lost many millions of factory jobs in ten years, should scare the politicians enough to rewrite the book on capitalism. Why hasn't it? Because politicians depend on the continuing largess of major American corporations which make far more profit by exporting our manufacturing jobs to countries with dollar-a-day labor. More profit to channel to business-friendly politicians. It's a closed loop and you and I don't figure into it at all.

So universities must be called on to take up the slack. They can develop and offer degrees in manufacturing science, emphasizing automation, robotics, time/motion studies, man/machine interface, labor psychology and qualifying for international certifications known as the ISO Standards. This new emphasis on manufacturing generated by our schools of higher learning will not only be good for our labor force, it will be of direct benefit to the schools themselves, creating a new revenue stream. How? To make the proposition more attractive to the schools, actual factories making real products could be built, while exploring, studying and improving the manufacturing process itself. These factories could be stand-alone university ventures or built in collaboration with small businesses. (I can hear the shrillness of the critics now. "But the universities would be competing against our own corporations! To which I reply: So what?). Maybe a kick in the butt is exactly what our over-indulged, over-protected corporate socialists need so they can figure out where their true interests lie.

If we change the way in which we think about domestic manufacturing to something positive and essential to our overall vitality as a nation, instead of as an old relic of an obsolete industrial age, we will find a huge reserve of good will and resources eager to re-energize our economy. I am not proposing protectionism. What I am saying is that we Americans have every right to provide for our own families, every right to rebuild and restore the manufacturing industry that once made us the power house of the world, every right to build the products we use, right here in this country. We do not owe the world an apology for providing for our own people. But aren't GE, Dell, HP, etc. our own people? Apparently not.

In addition to pumping more money into university research, I would enable the universities to create jobs by expanding their labs and workshops to produce the results of their research and development and sell them for a profit. This is not any different from the funding we lavish on the corporations to develop new products. The federal government has a long-standing policy of awarding contracts as small business set-asides. We can do the same or similar to restrict selected government contracts to universities with the caveat that all operations must stay within the U.S.

Following are some examples of university lab research into promising technologies for future development. The only question to be answered is why can't these technologies be sheltered as proprietary and licensed very selectively to a U.S.-only manufacturing base?

The University of Southern California, School of Engineering, has come up with a new way to collect and store solar energy in paper-thin organic photovoltaic sheets so unique that we may one day be able to charge our cell phones with the clothing we wear. The process lends itself to large-scale production, is light-weight and cheap to produce. No word on who would get the rights to use this technology. It's something our new Department of Domestic Research, Development and Manufacturing should be negotiating for.

At the Massachusetts Institute of Technology researchers are working on unique plastic acoustic fibers that can detect and produce sound. Variations on the concept could be used to measure blood flow in capillaries and blood pressure in the brain. Wouldn't the rest of the world be willing to buy such wondrous inventions? In the end, development of these technologies is paid for by the tax dollars of the American public. Aren't we entitled to reap some of the profits via creation of U.S. jobs? Why, why do we just casually give this technology away to whoever wants it?

A Seattle-based company which was spun out of the University of Washington received a $21.3 million grant from the Department of Energy to build a factory in Albany, Oregon, which will manufacture material for ultra capacitors that can be used to store energy in vehicles and on the electricity grid. More companies are R&Ding ultra capacitors for energy storage because they have different characteristics from batteries. Although batteries can store more energy, ultra capacitors can more quickly charge and discharge electrical energy plus they degrade very little over time.

The company does not plan to make the actual energy storage devices. To which I reply, why not? It sounds like a perfect job-creating manufacturing application to me. So will you perfect this new high-tech material on the U.S. Government's nickel and then sell the manufacturing rights to some company in China? O.K., O.K. I'm jumping the gun but in many, many cases this is exactly what happens. And just to take it full circle, who funds the Department of Energy? The tax revenues of you and me and millions of other American tax payers, 9.4% of whom have no jobs at this writing.

In Ohio, according to the Dayton Daily News, the president of Ohio State University said he'd like to see universities and private businesses partner on a fund to invest in new spin-off business opportunities jump-started from university research projects around the state. University officials are backing an idea to pool resources in a $100 million-plus venture capital fund. The core strategy is for helping the state grow via the development of research at the universities to create jobs for Ohioans. One of the limiting factors has been the lack of venture capital available. The new college-business partnership would help address this funding shortage. The idea has the support of the University of Dayton and several other Dayton-area universities.

In President Obama's State of the Union Address on January 27, 2011, he spoke of the need for American innovation. Mr. President, American innovation is happening all across our country. It is just not coming from our "great" American corporations anymore.

Follow the real innovation, Mr. President; it's happening right now in America's universities. That's where we need to invest. That's where our future lies if we are to have a prosperous future at all.

Where The Rubber Meets The Road

Let's talk about you and me. We are not responsible for everything. We did not get the country into this mess. But unfortunately, we can not just abruptly cut off all foreign trade. Today, all of our systems are interconnected. Any sudden dramatic change in economic policy anywhere on the globe reverberates around the world almost instantly affecting securities markets, currency valuations, increasing volatility in food stuffs, oil, gold, copper, etc. Our country has to start small and make gradual changes but there are things we as individuals can do; little things, big things, creative things, many of which have been discussed in these pages, all of which depend on adopting a different spirit toward our country and each other.

Reach out to your friends, family, neighbors and project a message of patriotism as Americans and ask them to join you in rejecting the phony, manipulating partisanship of the politicians, regardless of the party. Use the internet to identify, follow and encourage independent candidates for office.

Get involved in political discourse but be respectful of others ideas. Marshall your facts, stick to logical arguments, avoid name calling; that's for six-year olds. When we were young adults, (my generation) we used to stay up all night talking politics, careers, our place in the world, even religion, earnestly trying to change each other's points of view. And we always parted friends. We understood that it is o.k. to disagree without becoming abusive in our beliefs. Today's politics is so poisonous, so hateful, so over-the-top, it's hard to believe that we all still call ourselves "Americans".

When you go into a store to buy something, check to see where the product was made. You will be floored by how few products are still made in the U.S. and will reinforce your understanding that those products once represented the wages and wealth of a great nation, ours.

Try to find products still made in this country. There are some, usually made by small, local businesses and that's good. Those are precisely the companies we need to support. Keep our dollars within our own local communities where they can do the most good for Americans. Buy locally produced food. This list is potentially endless and can include everything from home-canned preserves to locally grown produce, fish and meats. Farmers markets are great sources of all kinds of local food, as are roadside produce stands. You might even grow some of your own vegetables and start a club to swap with other private gardeners (during WWII, we called them "victory gardens"). On vacation, consider staying at a local bed and breakfast instead of a conventional hotel chain. Paris Hilton doesn't need the money. If stocking up on alcohol, think about home-brewed beer, locally produced wines. Use the internet to locate local, Mom-and-Pop enterprises for all kinds of consumer products; hand-made clothes, hand-crafted furniture, leather goods, many different crafts. Also, there are many crafts fairs all around the country and you can again use the internet to find out where and when they meet. Instead of buying cheap imported goods which do nothing except drive up our deficit still higher, how about buying recycled goods from local yard sales, flea markets, estate sales, auctions, Good Will Industries, the Salvation Army. In most cases these products will cost pennies on the dollar, keep all that stuff out of landfills and keep those dollars at home. Forget the dollar stores. It's all imported junk. If we really want to send a message to the government and their multi-national corporate cronies, this is the way to do it. They will absolutely hate it. I guarantee it. And there's nothing they can do about it.

Talk up the goal of bringing manufacturing back to the U.S., especially production of new, cutting-edge technologies involving energy, water treatment, environmental conservation and agriculture science. These are needs which will never diminish and will in fact become more and more critical as world population continues to explode.

Then write to your congressman even if you think he can't read and demand the federal government stop making trade agreements. NO MORE TRADE AGREEMENTS!! Listen very carefully; free-trade agreements with foreign countries are and always will be a net loss for American jobs, that is until most Americans are making $1.00/hour like many of our poorest foreign neighbors. Then and only then will we reach parity with the rest of the world. It's the Law of Supply and Demand. If you think the politicians and corporate royalty don't know this, you are deceiving yourself. They know it and they do not care. It has no effect on their future earnings, only on yours.

Push the federal government to supply more comprehensive labeling of all products. Where did the product originate? What about the materials used to make the product? What country did they come from? Americans have a right to know what they are plunking down their hard-earned money for, the right to decide, based on the origin of the product, whether they want to buy one product over another. Some producing countries are known to have less safe products than others. China immediately springs to mind. They have a long and varied track record in producing harmful foods, drugs and toys. I would rather pay more for a product and feel confident that it's not going to hurt or kill me or my family.

We also need a better system for tracing back to the source of foods that have resulted in food poisoning. Some of the tainted food has ultimately been found to have been grown or produced right here in the U.S. but it has taken an unacceptably long time period to confirm this. Better labeling and record keeping could alleviate this lack. Gee, that might actually create some new jobs.

Recently, there have been suggestions that maybe we should split the Food and Drug Administration into two separate bureaus. So, then we could have two ineffective departments instead of just one. The answer is to give more regulatory power and more resources to the existing FDA. If foreign imports do not or can not comply with U.S. health standards, stop importing those products. Yes, it really is just that simple. With very few exceptions, there is absolutely no reason why our food and drugs can not be produced right here at home. Here's a scary fact; 80% of the ingredients in drugs consumed in the U.S. are imported from China or India. And yet, as we all know, the retail cost of drugs is astronomically high.

Currently, only about 1% of all imported food is inspected by the FDA. This is a task which could be contracted out to universities (make them the employers). It's not rocket science. College students could be paid to do the inspections, using pre-printed check lists. Many of them desperately need the funds to stay in school. Students could also be used to determine the validity of Medicare, Medicaid and Social Security claims through on-site inspections and interviews of claimants. In both cases, inspections would be unannounced spot checks.

In a slightly different vein, help each other as neighbors, volunteer at a soup kitchen, gather up excess clothes, toys and books and deliver them in person to a church pastor in the other part of town. Your unselfish charity, especially if you're feeling down on yourself, will lift your spirits. Guaranteed.

You young people ask a senior whose opinions you respect, not necessarily a family member, what it was like for them growing up. You might be surprised at the knowledge and wisdom that comes forth. And you might take advantage of the exchange to seek their advice on your employment pursuits.

Never stop learning. Never stop asking "why"? Never stop questioning your own assumptions about life. Life is a process and the process never ends. In your later years, you will be astonished by how much you sound just like your parents.

No one can do everything but everyone can do something to try to make our government work better. Find your niche. Is it letter writing? Organizing rallies? Protesting? Setting up web sites? Campaigning for (hopefully) independent candidates? Getting petitions signed? Marching on Washington? Getting your own "American jobs for Americans" bumper stickers printed up and distributed to friends and anyone else who accepts them? Or maybe it's just voicing a patriotic (but non-partisan) word now and then in defense of your own country. Go for it.

Power Blogging

There is enormous power in the collective will of the people once they focus on a single goal. Keep that thought in mind as we consider the mass communication power of the internet.

Throughout all of human history, we have never seen anything quite like the Internet. It's power, scope and reach is beyond measure. It has the potential to change the course of all humankind for good…or for evil. It can also serve as just another trinket in our toy box of diversions, one of its more popular uses.

In this chapter, let's consider how we can use the internet to locate like-minded individuals who want to unite to accomplish specific goals. Let me suggest a few topics well worth pursuing to achieve needed change in our economy and in our politics.

DEVELOPING AMERICA

Start a website where researchers, inventors and investors can find each other for the purpose of developing new ideas, new technologies and new products to benefit the U.S. industrial base. The ideas, of course, would not be discussed in detail on line but would serve as a point of introduction with additional data to be exchanged incrementally off-line until all parties are satisfied of legitimate intentions.

MADE IN THE USA

Start a web site where American manufacturers' can post their products provided that at least 65% of the materials and 100% of the manufacturing is U.S. originated. Producers should post the percentages along with their products. They know exactly where their products come from. The purpose of the website is to encourage Americans to support local manufacturing to the greatest extent possible. I would also encourage local producers to place on their products "Proudly made in _____ (your town/state) USA" and brag about your home town origins loudly and often. Heck, you could have bumper stickers made up and lavish them on your suppliers (American) and customers. We must bring pride in our products and each other back to this country. It is essential for our long-term survival. Foreign corporations need not be totally shut out. The key is where the product is manufactured. If the factory is in the U.S. using American labor, they may qualify.

INDEPENDENT GOVERNMENT

Start a website to identify independent candidates state by state to encourage these candidates to tell the people what they stand for (no, not lower taxes, smaller government and a free Cadillac for every citizen) but to propose realistic measures which can help grow the economy. Also write in whether or not your state holds open primaries. Closed primaries shut out that part of the electorate who choose to register as "independent".

UNREPRESENTATIVE GOVERNMENT

What about the primaries in your state? Are they open, closed, candidates chosen by caucus? You can become an armchair expert on your state's political structure and then report on it on your web site and invite comments from other citizens of your state. We must start reforming the way in which we choose our candidates for office. Closed state primaries and caucuses negate the democratic process and also work to keep the two major parties in power, to the exclusion of independent candidates with fresh ideas. These are things we can do on our own, in our own states, which would provide us satisfaction and a sense of accomplishment. Contact your state capital and request details on the nominating process for federal, state and local legislators. Find out how much of the political process is embedded in the two major parties, rather than in an independent and neutral government-sponsored program. It will be a real eye opener. Then publish your findings and invite other citizens from your state to add more research and plan how to make changes to your state's nominating process. Nothing scares the politicians more than activist citizens.

PIGGY CEO's

Start a website where people can write in about the most obscene pay packages of American CEO's that they are aware of. Name names, name companies and give the dollar details. As an added benefit, break it down into an hourly wage. You may be surprised to learn that many corporate CEO's make more money in one day than the average worker makes in an entire year. Find out the minimum wage for your state and list that also for comparison purposes. To take it even further, divide the minimum wage into that CEO's annual pay package to determine how many minimum wage workers could be paid with his wages. Who do you think is more likely to spend their entire paycheck into the local economy?

CREDIT UNIONS AND YOU

Start a website about your favorite credit union or locally-owned bank or savings & loan and tell why (interest rates, credit card rates, savings accounts, mortgage and auto loans, etc.) Also tell if they will under some circumstances, accept non-member applicants (ask them). The purpose of this is to make a determined effort to take down a peg the mega-bucks banks that almost destroyed the American economy. If you're waiting for congress to pass really tough legislation I have a few words for you "When hell…

IT'S THE JOBS, STUPID

I'll go first. I've started a website about this book and I'm soliciting input. I've named it, rather brilliantly I thought, Itsthejobsstupid.com. All reasoned opinions welcomed. There are no good or bad opinions. There is only apathy.

It's All About You, Honest

Over the years, I've had a fair amount of success at finding jobs. I've moved around a lot (long story), so quite often I was seeking a job in a new locale. I have developed opinions on what works and what doesn't and if you are currently seeking employment you might find some of these experiences helpful.

I have never found employment agencies to be particularly useful in my job searches. If you have outstanding credentials, you don't need them. If you don't, an employment agency isn't going to help you. They are in business to make a profit, just like any other business, and they will reach for the resumes that contain the cream of the crop, every time.

Where I would invest some time and effort (and dollars of course) is with a professional resume writer. Especially if you are fresh out of college with little work experience, a resume writer can coax your hidden talents out of you and commit them to paper. I used a professional with great success. He made my limited accomplishments sparkle and I did, in fact, land several jobs with my creatively-embellished resume. I never would have had the nerve to write anything so flamboyant, but as I said, it worked! And it was all true. It's just a matter of accentuating the positive.

Speaking about work experience (or the lack of) we all think we're too good to work at those low-pay jobs that are always available and nobody wants like cashiering, waitressing, bartending, burger slinging, house cleaning and so on but some experience of any kind is better than no experience in anything. Even perfect attendance counts.

About those resumes, if you mail out (yes, mail out not email) twenty resumes and stop, don't expect to find a job. You need to send out 500-700 copies of your resume to have a reasonable chance of reply. In mass mailings of any kind, the rate of reply is approximately 1%. The good news is those five to seven responses tend to be serious inquiries. If you can't whip up the energy to do this on your own, there are resume services which will do the whole thing for you, for a fee naturally.

Network, network, network. The experts say that up to 70% of job openings are never advertised in the local paper and the ones which are, are inundated with a ton of resumes. Your chances of getting to the first interview are really slim. If you take the path less traveled, your chances of landing a job automatically increase. So, talk to the people around you; friends, distant relatives, neighbors, local merchants like your hairdresser, sports bartender, anyone with a pulse. Also, pull out your local phone book and start shooting out resumes to local businesses. Someone out there has been thinking about hiring a new employee for quite some time and then your resume shows up in the mail! The employer really doesn't want to advertise and slog through hundreds of resumes and you seem as though you could do a good job. What good luck! For both of you!

Many employment experts recommend that you research each company you plan to apply to and write a cover letter tailored to that company. I strongly disagree. You should write a cover letter, yes, and you should make it as strong as possible conveying the generic strengths you bring to the table. But your cover letter should itself be a form letter into which you simply add the name, address and salutation of the company you are writing to. There are a number of reasons to go this route. In today's challenging economy, there aren't that many jobs available and it doesn't matter if your cover letter is Shakespeare, if there are no jobs, there are no jobs. Secondly, the time and sheer effort of composing all those fancy and unique cover letters will break your heart. It's a numbers game. Treat it as such. Don't take it personally. It will eat you up. Look at it as a business transaction, one of many you will have to negotiate throughout your career.

On the subject of personal walk-ins to prospective employers, make a list of companies and businesses in your immediate area, an easy driving distance from your home and then on the first clear weather day, make the rounds and talk to as many employers as you can get close to. At a minimum, ask for an employment application which you can take with you for "future opportunities". Then fill it out, wait two or three weeks and then hand-deliver it back and request to see the hiring manager to introduce yourself. All they can say is "no". Don't take any rejection personally. Develop a tough skin. With practice, you will, and this newly developed skill will also serve you well as you move through your career.

Attend every local job fair you can find. It's a chance to get face time with a potential employer and businesses which interview through job fairs actually have jobs to fill or they wouldn't invest the time. At a minimum, it's worth getting some practice in front of a real employer and at least you will learn what's out there.

Other possibilities to think about; consider part-time or temporary work which can sometimes lead to an offer for full-time permanent employment. Consider night work, even if just temporarily. Hotels, hospitals, bus and taxi drivers, long distance freight haulers all require night shifts. Consider applying for a federal government civil service position. The feds maintain offices in every major city in the country and they are always hiring some people even in the worst of times like now. One caution: You may have to take a civil service exam to be considered for federal employment. Also you will have to apply to the federal departments individually. There is no one central hiring agency.

Last but not least consider telling the prospective employer that you will work for free to prove your worth as an employee. This too succeeded for me in landing a job. I told a dubious employer I would work for the company free for two weeks to prove I could handle the job. He was so impressed by my determination that he hired me immediately, at full pay. I was with the company for two years.

Perhaps you've already tried all these things and you think I'm pretty lame for putting such basic ideas in a book. Fair enough. I have to admit that in finding a job, there is always an element of luck involved. You have to be at the right place at the right time. How will you know where and when that is? You won't if you just make the rounds in person for one day and then give up or if you just send out twenty resumes and then go shoot hoops with your friends. The people I know who eventually found jobs treated their employment search as if it were their full-time job. They kept at it, pretty much all day, every day, until they got an offer and then they accepted the offer, even if it wasn't what they really wanted.

Finally, even though employed, they kept looking for that perfect job. It is easier to find a job when you don't need one. You are in a much stronger bargaining position. You know it. And the prospective employer knows it too.

So keep at it and you will succeed.

Don't Get Mad, Get Even

Is there anyone left out there who doesn't know how badly the banks and Wall Street screwed us over with this sub-prime mortgage mess? Personally, I was in favor of sending in the government auditors and taking over the banks and firing all of the top management (and investigating for criminal fraud). I wouldn't have given them a penny. The line that nobody could have foreseen the looming crisis is just crap. What did they think was going to happen when the payments on those balloon mortgages doubled? By 2004-05 a few savvy economists and reporters were already projecting the coming calamity as were a few federal regulators. They were ignored, even discredited, by Greenspan and the Bush White House.

As Americans struggle to overcome their losses, we may want to revisit the financial relationships we have with some of these mega-bucks predators, namely, Bank of America (aka: F.I.A. Card Services), Citibank, American Express, (J.P. Morgan) Chase, Wells Fargo, Capital One. Notwithstanding new legislation which is designed to rein in the most egregious practices of the banking/credit industry, we find that these corporations are just inventing new ways to ensnare average consumers. You may have already heard of or experienced the $35.00 cup of coffee due to overcharging on your debit card.

One of the most effective and most satisfying strategies we can employ to get off the credit treadmill is to work at paying off and permanently closing the accounts we maintain with these "too big to fail" mega-crooks. And by the way, we can direct these companies to close our accounts now even while we still have a balance due. We may find this action particularly useful because these credit card companies are now starting to charge "inactivity" fees. That's right, keeping these accounts open is a lose-lose situation because they may start charging you a penalty for not using your account. Of course, we will still be held responsible to pay off the balance and we will no longer be able to charge to the account but there are better alternatives.

I suggest investigating local credit unions. On line, search for "credit unions". Select the main site and then enter your zip code. You should get a pop-up list of credit unions in your community. Why credit unions? These organizations which are member-owned and supported have many advantages, starting with typically lower interest rates. Many of them offer all of the same services as banks including checking accounts, savings accounts, loans for cars, mortgages. Many offer their own credit cards, again at typically lower rates and without the hidden "gotcha" fees we've come to loath from the big crooks. But with respect to credit cards, make sure they are self-funding the cards and not just shilling for Bank of America. Ask who finances their credit cards.

Credit unions tend to be smaller than banks but not to worry. Deposits are guaranteed just like those of bank savings accounts by deposit insurance of at least $250,000 per member through the National Credit Union Share Insurance Fund. This deposit insurance is administered by the National Credit Union Administration. U.S. credit unions have approximately 90 million members. Credit unions don't usually advertise themselves in splashy TV ads so you may not have even thought of them. But the peace of mind that comes from feeling that you are finally in control of your own finances - priceless.

Some credit unions have a closed membership based on unique criteria however, other unions have opened up their membership in the quest for new business. So shop around, ask lots of questions. Just think of the satisfaction you'll feel in telling the finance crooks you're taking your business elsewhere.

One last thought, try to pay cash for your smaller purchases. It sounds so obvious. And it is so much easier to whip out a card, credit or debit. You know how many dollars you need to get through the week. If you don't, start a list. Once you have a number for the lunches, dry cleaners and coffees, take that much money out in cash when you deposit your paycheck. This exercise may even prompt you to start packing a lunch but that's a whole other subject.

On a personal, strictly selfish note, I hate to receive gift cards. It's a hassle to redeem them. They usually lay around til they expire and then I feel guilty for squandering a well-intended gift. But you just can't beat the convenience and versatility of folding money. Ask some older people which they would rather receive, cash or a gift card. I bet I know the answer.

Make Them Work For It

Winston Churchill (1874-1965) the famous and courageous British Prime Minister during World War II, was also an author and noted wit. He once told a critical temperance lady, "I may be drunk, Miss, but in the morning, I will be sober and you will still be ugly". More relevant to our discussion here, Churchill also once said, "You can always count on Americans to do the right thing, after they've tried everything else". Nowhere is our American shortsightedness more evident than in the American tax code.

It is often said, usually by members of congress, that the federal government does not create jobs, that job creation is within the purview of the private sector. Fair enough. But there is plenty the feds can do to make it unpleasant for American corporations to keep sending our factories and jobs overseas, while rewarding investment in domestic businesses. (Make the distinction between manufacturing jobs and exports. We want to keep the factories and jobs here, but export the maximum goods possible.) The federal government knows full well how to influence taxpayer behavior through adjustments in tax incentives. As previously mentioned, the Earned Income Tax Credit, passed during the Clinton administration, encouraged low-earning citizens to continue working instead of applying for welfare. More recently, the feds have initiated tax credits to buyers of new homes, new cars and energy-efficient appliances and equipment in order to stimulate the economy. These last tax breaks benefited mainly middle class taxpayers. Americans are very familiar with the concept of quid pro quo, something for something, one thing in return for another. It's the basis of our capitalist system.

But when it comes to the super-rich and mega-corporations, it's almost as though the feds don't want to offend anybody by offering tax incentives for investing in America, for hiring American workers, for manufacturing products here instead of in some foreign country. No, our tax cuts to the rich are a dead loss with no reciprocity, no strings attached, no quid pro quo. Then we wonder why the hoity-toitys keep sending their investment dollars overseas. Year after year, decade after decade, our government defends a tax system that is rigged to continuously benefit the rich at the expense of average Americans, who are, in truth, where most of those tax dollars come from.

Many in congress claim that we must keep taxes to the rich low because the rich invest and create jobs. The rich create jobs alright. In the Philippines. In Sri Lanka. In South Korea. In Malaysia. In Indonesia. But not here. Case in point: According to a recent 2011 newspaper article, call center jobs now account for 350,000 employees in the Philippines, topping the 330,000 employees in India. That will be acceptable to most Americans until they realize that these call centers are fielding calls from American customers located in the U.S. and the corporations paying these foreign-based call centers are also American. That's 680,000 jobs which could have been filled by Americans, who could have been paying income and payroll taxes to the U.S. Treasury. And by the way, the Philippines and Indian call centers generated $6.3 Billion and $5.6 Billion respectively in revenue last year for them, not us. Among the American companies represented are Citi and J.P. Morgan Chase and other banks, insurance companies, telecom and computer technology firms. The reason for the increase in using employees in the Philippines is that these companies know Americans increasingly resent the off-shoring of so many American jobs so they are trying to hide the fact of off-shoring by using the speech skills of the most accent-neutral country, the Philippines. So if you can not detect a foreign accent the next time you talk to your credit card company, you may still be talking to an employee half-way around the world. According to this same article, English-speaking employees in Manila also do research, process claims, develop software and do accounting, all for American flag-waving, U.S.-based corporations.

The rich invest to make more profit. Period. And more and more, those investments are going overseas to emerging market countries like Brazil, Russia, India and China (in Wall Street parlance known as the BRIC's). The rich have no intention of investing just to underwrite the progress of America. There simply is not enough profit in it anymore. And forget any sense of patriotism. The hoity-toity rich may not even consider themselves American citizens any more, even if they were born and raised here. They likely consider themselves as "citizens of the world" along with their rich counter-parts from other countries and a royal or two. Once they have finished gutting the United States, they will simply retire to their rehabbed castles in Scotland or Spain or to their chateaus in France. Congress knows all this and does nothing. Or just calls for another tax cut for the rich, who, after all, finance the politicians' reelections in perpetuity. Many members of congress are themselves, hoity-toity interns, so why would they want to raise their own tax rates?

The United States is a country of 311 million citizens. How does it feel to be competing against a world population of seven billion people? In most of these countries, workers are eager, skills are plentiful and deprivation has been endemic for so long, any steady wage-paying job is like year-round Christmas. And not all the products these countries are making are rubber spears or paper parasols. Not anymore. Think semiconductors, ever more sophisticated hardware and software, even stealth bombers. China already has a high-speed bullet train that puts anything we have to shame. So just what is our competitive advantage going forward? What is our value added? Why should anybody buy anything from the United States when they can buy it a lot closer to home? And cheaper? And our universities? Several books have been written in recent years on the subject of the growing internationalization of higher education generally and American university science and research more particularly. Again, where do we go from here?

If the definition of insanity is doing the same thing over and over again while expecting a different result, at least half the members of the U.S.

House and Senate should be committed. Soon. Or maybe it's just time to do the right thing. We've already tried everything else.

We need to put teeth back into the "Buy American Act", especially when it concerns direct government purchases. Where does that money come from in the first place? It comes from the American taxpayer. So why does the U.S. Government buy everything from jock straps to floating dry docks from foreign countries all around the globe? That money needs to stay here and provide revenue for American small businesses and American workers. "Buy American" for purchases by our government should not be a suggestion, it should be a requirement, as it once was.

We need tax cuts targeted to those who invest in America. There's a lot of talk about "simplifying" the tax code. Not gonna happen. Every time the feds dink around with the tax code, it winds up more complicated, not less. We're lucky we don't end up with something like the idiot Forbe's 15% flat tax or George Will's proposed abolishment of the minimum wage. (Yeah, what you guys do to make a living is so, so vital to our economy.) So let's take advantage of the complexities of the tax code to spell out how the mega-rich can significantly reduce their tax rates. How? By investing in America, of course. This would be quite apart from the usual tax credits for investing and would require a different form. After all the credits and all the deductions were tallied and a preliminary tax estimated, the taxpayer could select from a number of domestic-only programs which the feds would designate and pledge to invest a certain dollar amount. These programs could include hiring more employees, investing in product research and development, opening new factories, etc. In exchange, the investor could see his next year's tax rate decreased by some percent or fractional percentage.

Advantages of implementing a tax credit in this way are that it would be voluntary and it would be private, between the government and the tax payer (although it might be problematic in the case of publicly-traded corporations), so it needn't set off protectionist alarm bells in every foreign country from here to Beijing. Hell, give me, a private citizen, the option of designating my tax dollars to U.S.-only programs and I will check that box every time. Why? Because every dollar invested in America-only enterprise means more tax dollars which ultimately come back to benefit me, whether in more medical research, infrastructure improvements, better education, more police and firemen, or lower taxes for everyone.

Of course, none of this stuff will happen if all we do is grumble to each other. We need to complain directly to the politicians. Complain loudly, repeatedly and not just at election time. Make a pest out of yourself. It's o.k. This is America. Send those emails, invest in that postage stamp, call your senator and representative. If you don't know who they are, go to www.senate.gov and www.house.gov for complete lists of our elected officials.

Do the right thing.

Insane Or Not

I'm not an economist and don't pretend to be but let's not strain ourselves to make this more complicated than is. To suggest that lowering taxes increases tax revenues is ridiculous on the face of it, especially since this country has been running a large and ever increasing federal deficit with China since 1985 and as we've pointed out, the use of other peoples' money is not free (unless you're Wall Street). So the question is at what point do the interest charges on the national debt wipe out our entire gross domestic product? We're making really great progress on that, if in fact that is the goal. According to a statement made recently on TV by a U.S. senator, we now borrow .40 cents of every dollar we spend.

However, it appears that the surest way to get defeated in an election is to preside over an increase in taxes as George Bush (the elder) found out in 1992 when he ran for reelection against Bill Clinton. (Clinton raised taxes too.) But I'm not running for public office nor do I intend to be and I promised to tell the truth so I will declare vehemently that insane or not, we must raise taxes on all Americans. The government is not collecting sufficient revenue in taxes to sustain critical public services. We are subsisting on a huge and ever growing annual federal deficit which in the end, will devour us. Our federal debt at the end of Clinton's term was 56.4% of our gross domestic product. At the end of George W. Bush's term (the younger) it was 83.4% of GDP. We must keep in mind that for much of the 20th century, our top marginal tax rates hovered between 90% and 60%. It is worth repeating that it was in the eighties at the insistence of Ronald Reagan that our top tax rates dropped to 28% and our economy has since experienced a virtual free-fall largely because of the wildly lopsided policies he initiated. No wonder Reagan was such a popular president. Especially with the rich.

Even Alan Greenspan, the former chief of the Federal Reserve has stated that never before have we been in this position. He was referring most particularly to the jobless recovery of 2010. But he also said we must clean up our act, economically speaking, if we are to continue to have the capacity to borrow. Pause for a moment and consider what that would mean for your household. If you don't have the cash and you don't have sufficient income to cover your basic living expenses, you're only other alternative is to borrow. But once you've maxed out on your credit and can no longer borrow, what do you do? You're looking at default, possibly bankruptcy. You could lose your home, your car, everything you own. Greenspan is saying our country is close to this most critical juncture, beyond which we dare not go. Why not? Because our economy will collapse and chaos will ensue. We will pray for the return of a mere 10% unemployment. Unlike our Euro-zone friends across the pond, there will be no one to bail us out.

The tax-cut extension passed by congress at the end of 2010 and the weak economy will add 1.5 Trillion Dollars to the 2011 federal deficit according to the latest estimate by congressional budget analysts. This represents the largest budget short-fall in U.S. history. We can expect a similar short-fall in 2012 and since we are already broke, the total will be tacked onto our $14 Trillion-plus long-term debt as we have been doing with all our unfunded federal liabilities. The tax-cut extension applies across the board even to the super rich but it will expire in 2012 which guarantees the issue will come up again during the next presidential election year.

During the 2010 debate on extending the tax cuts, the Democrats favored for the most part extending the tax cuts only on those making less than $250 thousand a year. The Republicans in congress said that raising taxes on those making more than $250 thousand a year would cripple the recovery of the economy by punishing small business owners and preventing them from hiring employees. This argument is inaccurate in so many ways, on so many levels, it is difficult to know where to start. Let's start with the stuff that is easiest to refute. The Democrats lost the argument over raising taxes on small business owners who create jobs. But what about extending the tax cuts to multi-millionaires and billionaires? The Democrats never posed the question, rather stupidly, I thought. So the tax breaks were extended across the board to millionaires and billionaires. ($20 for you, $200,000 for me, $2 Million for him.) Also, some in congress glibly spout off about personal income and business income as though they were the same thing and interchangeable. They are not. Very different rules apply, even within small businesses and even within small business corporate structures sometimes known as Subchapter S Corporations. Tax payers who have never owned their own business may not be aware of the distinctions but members of congress certainly are and they use phony devices like this to cloud the issues and confuse the public.

Let's delve a little deeper into this $250 Thousand figure that everyone was talking about in 2010 and let's quantify it for personal tax purposes and for business tax purposes. In the first place, taxpayers earning approximately $250,000 a year are far more likely to be high net worth individuals, such as actors, athletes, authors, lawyers and yes, politicians, rather than a small, labor intensive business such as a factory (which scarcely exists anymore except overseas). In the second place, all businesses of any size and self-employed individuals as noted above, have the right to do something the typical wage earner may not do which is to deduct all of the expenses related to the production of revenue from the gross income. The earnings or profit remaining after deducting all the expenses may be significantly less than $250,000 in taxable income. In some cases expenses may exceed gross revenues altogether therefore, there's no taxable income at all. It is the mitigating effects of deductions which enables Warren Buffet to claim, accurately, that he pays less in taxes, proportionately, than his secretary does (Warren Buffet was our country's second-richest citizen in 2010).

Finally, there is a real difference between marginal tax rates on which our tax system is based, and the generic or average tax rates commonly referred to in general conversation. It is easy to come to the conclusion that someone earning $500,000/year will pay the top tax rate, currently 35% on the whole $500K or $175,000. This is not accurate. The marginal tax rate is the rate on the last dollar earned. Even with no deductions, a 35% tax bracket applies only to earnings above $155,975, to use a recent example. Earnings on the first $7000 would be taxed at the $7000 rate, which, using our example, would be 10%, exactly the same rate as any other citizen would pay. The next $14,400 would be taxed at 15% again, the same as any other taxpayer would pay. It is not until we reach six figure incomes that the higher tax rates kick in and they top out at 35%. (Figures are for demonstration purposes only. Tax regulations change year to year. Consult your tax professional - not me.) It doesn't matter if the taxpayer is a millionaire or billionaire. Furthermore, because of the many deductions legally available to businesses and the self-employed, even under a Subchapter S Corporation, their taxable income after deductions is likely much lower than that of a wage earner, assuming the same dollars in gross income. Again, think Warren Buffet, one of only a handful of honest and patriotic wealthy Americans who said, "There are only two ways the government can collect its taxes; they can get it from me or from the person who serves me lunch". Buffet also guesstimated that he and his counterparts only pay between 16% and 17% of their annual income in taxes.

We could go on with this litany of taxes favoring the already rich. There's the capital gains tax rate which tops out at 15% for most gains no matter how rich the recipients are. There's the payroll tax (social security) another non-progressive tax shared by employee and employer alike to the tune of over 15% combined (includes Medicare) but that too tops out at $106,800 annual income even though social security revenue has been dipped into and depleted for decades to finance the war du jour in order to pander to the military-industrial-governmental revolving Washington door. And the much-maligned social security system is the only federal entitlement that has its own separate revenue stream yet the funds have never been kept separate from general tax revenues. So in essence, the payroll tax deduction for social security amounts to a stealth tax which falls particularly hard on the lower middle-class and the working poor.

And now the Bowles-Simpson Commission on Reducing the National Debt which reported its findings at the end of 2010, wants to eliminate the home mortgage deduction, probably the last refuge of the wage-earning middle class. Some are even suggesting drastic cuts to social security or even abolishment. Let Grandma starve.

It seems like every time the feds talk about ways to increase revenue, the middle class gets bitch-slapped with the bill. And the rich? They are untouchable. I have to admit the Teabaggers have a right to be angry. I am told that the "Tea" stands for "Taxed Enough Already". And compared to the rich, they sure as hell are.

While it is impossible for the average taxpayer to follow the tortuous twists and turns of our tax system to understand who's paying his fair share of taxes and who's getting away with murder, let me repeat: to state that cutting taxes increases tax revenue is an absurd and outrageous lie. That's like saying 2+2 = 7. If a taxpayer is somehow hiding his income, he is breaking the law and we must deal with that situation, not reward him by further lowering his taxes. Yes, the issue is more complicated than that. Many books have been written on the dynamics of our capitalist system but those books dealt with a healthy capitalist system in which all the components of investment, production, profit and re-investment, etc. were mainly controlled and confined within one independent system, i.e. the United States and where supply and demand largely balanced out, again, within the same system. Anyone who has read this far in the book knows by now that ours is no longer a healthy capitalist system, and if we continue down this same road, will result in the destruction of our economy and ultimately our cherished Constitutional government.

Rewrite the tax code. We've spent far too many years tinkering around the edges and every time congress enacts another deduction or across-the-board tax cut of even a few percent, the rich get to buy another chateau in France, the middle class gets to take a vacation - to the in-laws. And the poor get to buy a few extra burgers at McDonald's. But we're all created equal, right?

Our current top marginal tax rate of 35% is just too low. It should be between 45% and 50%, at least until the federal debt is back to manageable levels. I have nothing to base this on except past tax rates and my gut. I'd be very curious to hear a serious discussion about it by economists, not politicians. Make the tax rates more progressive especially at the higher end. Current tax rates of 10, 25, 28, 33 and 35% hit the middle class disproportionately. Abolish the alternative minimum tax which is just another stealth tax on the middle class and it's dishonest.

The higher marginal tax rates should represent a more equitable distribution such that they do not kick in on incomes below $300,000. To be honest, in today's economy, $250,000 in annual income for a family of four is just not a lot of money. Think college for two kids. Also, if we want to encourage small business start-ups, personal, disposable income is one way to do it. But the difference between a millionaire and a billionaire is huge. This is where the top marginal tax rates need to be scaled up to 35, 45, even 50% to reflect the huge differences in income.

In a growing, thriving economy everybody reaps the rewards. People are not overly focused on pinching every penny or denying the government its fair share. Meanness, stinginess and greed are the legacy of a declining economy, as well as the understanding of the people that they are not being treated fairly or equally. Back to that cherry pie again, remember? There are only so many pieces to go around. If a couple of people hog the whole pie…

It doesn't matter if you're talking about a pie or a 14 trillion dollar economy. The arithmetic is the same. It's a zero sum game.

Enlightened Self-Interest

The philosophy of enlightened self-interest, posits that by helping along the interests of others, we ultimately serve our own self-interests. This is not to suggest that we should all be purely altruistic. Altruism calls for people to act in the service of others even when to do so may be detrimental to their own well-being. I think we can safely stipulate that most of us are not versions of Mother Teresa. No, enlightened self-interest is more of a quid pro quo proposition in the pure capitalist tradition or "I'll scratch your back if you scratch mine". Its opposite is the greedy, self-centered, single-minded selfishness model which is often successful short-term but ultimately fails as other people react to the selfish person's maneuvers resulting in loss of efficiency, continuing conflicts, ensuing backlash, and increased vigilance and expense as others move to protect their own interests. (Sounds like the United States Congress, doesn't it?)

Enlightened self-interest is also a fancy way of saying, what goes around, comes around. If you treat other people shabbily on the way to your self-centered goals and think it doesn't matter, you may be in for a big surprise when you encounter those same people who now have the upper hand. The problem with acting in total self-interest is we assume the other person will continue to act rationally, in a fair-minded way. No wonder the divorce rate is so high.

With the crash of the financial markets, loss in home values and steep rises in credit interest rates or no credit at all, Americans are facing a crisis of confidence in all our traditional institutions and yet, we are searching for something, anything, to believe in. Which may be why so many Americans have turned to God for reassurance. That's fine. But while it may be true that we can move mountains with God, let me suggest that we better bring a big-ass shovel. And since all we have on this earth is each other, perhaps God would want us to cooperate with each other in getting that mountain moving? It would be a way of honoring Him, yes?

It is not possible to overestimate the importance of restoring public confidence in the American system and in the totality of our institutions; financial, governmental and social. Young people especially, are anxious and angry at the prospect of graduating from college deep in debt due to student loans and being unable to find employment that covers much more than their loan payments. Kids who couldn't scrape together enough money to go to college are worse off. They're looking at the prospect of no prospects at all which will lead inevitably to drugs, homelessness, and lawlessness.

Throughout all of human history, great nations have risen; the Egyptians, the Greeks, the Roman Empire, the British Empire. They lived their day in the sun then crumbled, subverted by the excesses of their own people, into the ashes of their times. Early in the twentieth century the United States saw its fortunes and influence steadily rise to that of the world's first true super-power and we grew arrogant in our belief that we would always flourish, always triumph, exactly as the great empires before us came to believe. But reality, hard, raw, reality, has a way of reasserting itself. No matter how much the politicians lie, no matter how hard they try to deny the fact of our national decline, reality stubbornly refuses to yield. The last few years have shown us that our continued ascendancy in the world is not pre-determined. But surely our continued survival as a nation is guaranteed? No, it isn't. Once again, man's greed, ignorance and arrogance is foreshadowing his own undoing and the American people of today are the most arrogant, spoiled, self-centered, over-indulged, under-achieving group of people the world has ever known who have basically created and deserve the dysfunctional government they now have. Not you and me, of course. Other people.

So is it too late for our United States? That depends.

If we continue to squabble over our politician-magnified and largely illusionary political differences instead of combining our talents and playing to our national strengths, we don't have a prayer.

If we allow congress to continue rewarding big corporations for off-shoring our jobs and at the same time legislatively continue to favor foreign investment by these same companies, the U.S. employment base will continue to shrink meaning more unemployment, less tax revenues and more social unrest.

If we continue to cut taxes especially for the richest among us, we will continue to increase the federal deficit and there is a very real possibility that the U.S. economy will simply collapse under the sheer weight of its debts and we won't recover from the chaos in our lifetime.

If we continue to consume everything we can get our hands on without first making, creating, building, preserving, growing, for our own people, within our own borders, we shall see the day when the U.S.A. as we know it, ceases to exist. An economy based on consumer spending is no damned economy at all.

Finally, if we continue to place our civic education and responsibility somewhere south of our manicures, football stats and air guitar lessons, don't be surprised if some day soon a dictator sets up housekeeping in the White House permanently.

If you doubt any of the claims made in these pages, and given today's tortured truth you probably should, don't just go away with your cynicism intact. Please take some time to do your own research and get the unpoliticized, unmarketed, unmanipulated, unspun, unadvertised objective facts and make up your own mind about where our country is headed and what we need to do to pull it back from the abyss and reestablish our control over a truly representative government. All you need is a computer, a search engine and a bunch of key words.

It's your future. Do you really want somebody, anybody else to make the decisions for you?

Postscript

As I come to the end of this book, Jared Loughner is making court appearances in the murder of six Tucson, Arizona citizens and the wounding of their U.S. Representative, Gabby Giffords. I want to state unequivocally that nothing in this book should be construed as encouraging violence against our government and its elected officials.

Rather, this is a call to ballots, not bullets, a call to find like-minded citizens on the internet or elsewhere, to organize, to campaign, to support independent candidates who will support us, or to become a candidate for office yourself, to educate yourself about your government and finally, to cast a vote informed by your own independent research.

In a country where our government is still chosen by the people, it's the least we can do.

As long as we still have that privilege.

Appendix A

Methodology & Acknowledgments

In the majority of non-fiction "issues" publications, a long, very detailed source list is given to support the facts and figures cited throughout the book. I have not done that.

The federal government has made enormous progress in making information about its activities available to the public on-line. Much of the data cited in this book came from the government's own web sites including:

www.constitution.net
www.census.gov (Bur. Of the Census)
www.irs.gov (Internal Revenue Service)
www.treasury.gov (US Treasury Dept.)
www.dol.gov (Dept. of Labor)(click Bur. Of Labor Statistics)
www.senate.gov (US Senate)
www.house.gov (US House of Representatives)
www.whitehouse.gov
www.socialsecurity.gov
www.cbo.gov (Congressional Budget Office)
www.omb.gov (office of Mgmt. & Budget)

I encourage the reader to take advantage of this free and factual information which is available with a few keystrokes.

Beyond that, facts were obtained from the news media and television political commentary and then confirmed from independent sources, many on-line. These include:

Wall Street Journal
Washington Post
New York Times
Business Week
USA Today
Regional and local newspapers
ABC News
CBS News
NBC News
Fox News Sunday (Fox)
PBS News Hour
The McLaughlin Group (PBS)
Front Line (PBS)
Washington Week (PBS)
Bloomberg.com
This Week (ABC)
Meet the Press (NBC)
Nightly Business Report (PBS)
Google Search Engine
Wikipedia

I think you have been surprised, as I was, by some of the findings. Nonetheless, the book represents eight months of exhaustive research with many facts confirmed from multiple sources.

I did not use data, and do not recommend trying to get objective facts from partisan political talk shows, either liberal or conservative. These hate peddlers, whether on TV or radio, have a political agenda and they routinely spin reality or outright lie. Their business is selling anger and resentment which, it turns out, is very profitable. For them. Don't buy into it.

Finally, I have gone way past the facts and figures stage to make very specific allegations and recommendations. These are totally mine and I take responsibility for any fall-out.

Appendix B

DARPA's Organization

As discussed previously, the Defense Advanced Research Projects Agency is organized to maximize the laser-like focus on its technological goals. This is the same kind of dynamic, forward-thinking research and development which is desperately needed to incentivize break-throughs in the private sector. But where we need to deviate from the DARPA model is in limiting the use of the technologies to U.S.-based enterprises, notably small companies which will hire local talent and operate within the U.S. We absolutely do want to export hi-tech products which add revenue to our treasury. But we should not be exporting our hard-won and very-expensive-to-develop technological know-how which is exactly what we're doing right now. Once we teach other countries how to do it, they compete against us, and build it cheaper. We are committing economic suicide.

Following is the highly successful DARPA model:

DARPA ORGANIZATIONAL MODEL

- Small and flexible; DARPA has only about (140) technical professionals, sometimes referred to as "a hundred geniuses connected by a travel agent".

- Flat organization; DARPA avoids hierarchy, operating for the most part at only two management levels to enhance information flow and speed up decision-making.

- Autonomy; DARPA is not bound by the federal civil service hiring provisions, by design, and is able to make direct hires of technically talented individuals.

- World-class technical staff; DARPA uses the multi-talents of industry, university and government, laboratories and individuals, combining the theoretical, the experimental, the practical. DARPA does not own or operate its own facilities, hence the majority of the research it sponsors is performed in university and industry labs.

- Teams and networking; DARPA strives to create teams of researchers, talented in different disciplines who collaborate and share their expertise for the benefit of all.

- Hiring and change; DARPA's technical staff is assigned for four to six years, while mixing experience and dynamic change. Staff is rotated to encourage fresh thinking and new members are often added to the mix. Program managers are encouraged to be bold and able to risk failure in the pursuit of an important break-through.

- Project-based assignments organized around a challenge model; Some DARPA initiatives are organized for a specific technology challenge. They foresee a new, innovation-based capability and then work backward to achieve the all-important technical breakthroughs to make the new innovation possible.

- Most projects last three to five years, however, major technology initiatives may prompt longer-term investment and keep teams together for on-going collaboration. Continued funding by DARPA may be based on passing specific, incremental milestones.

- Emphasis on revolutionary breakthroughs; DARPA's focus has been on radical innovation. It emphasizes investment in high-risk initiatives, proceeds rapidly from research to prototype, then transfers further development and manufacturing to the private sector.

This data and much more can be found on the DARPA web site (www. DARPA.mil) and via computer search. It is my understanding that DARPA also has its own Facebook page.

Appendix C

F.D.R.'s Inaugural Address 1933

"I am certain that my fellow Americans expect that on my induction into the Presidency I will address them with a candor and a decision which the present situation of our Nation impels. This is preeminently the time to speak the truth, the whole truth, frankly and boldly. Nor need we shrink from honestly facing conditions in our country today. This great nation will endure as it has endured, will revive and prosper. So, first of all, let me assert my firm belief that the only thing we have to fear is fear itself--nameless, unreasoning, unjustified terror which paralyzes needed efforts to convert retreat into advance. In every dark hour of our national life a leadership of frankness and vigor has met with that understanding and support of the people themselves which is essential to victory. I am convinced that you will again give that support to leadership in these critical days.

In such a spirit on my part and on yours we face our common difficulties. They concern, thank God, only material things. Values have shrunken to fantastic values; taxes have risen; our ability to pay has fallen; government of all kinds is faced by serious curtailment of income; the means of exchange are frozen in the currents of trade; the withered leaves of industrial enterprise lie on every side; farmers find no markets for their produce; the savings of many years in thousands of families are gone.

More important, a host of unemployed citizens face the grim problem of existence, and an equally great number toil with little return. Only a foolish optimist can deny the dark realities of the moment.

Yet our distress comes from no failure of substance. We are stricken by no plague of locusts. Compared with the perils which our forefathers conquered because they believed and were not afraid, we still have much to be thankful for. Nature still offers her bounty and human efforts have multiplied it. Plenty is at our doorstep, but a generous use of it languishes in the very sight of the supply. Primarily this is because rulers of the exchange of mankind's goods have failed, through their own stubbornness and their own incompetence, have admitted their failure and abdicated. Practices of the unscrupulous money changers stand indicted in the court of public opinion, rejected by the hearts and minds of men.

True, they have tried, but their efforts have been cast in the pattern of an outworn tradition. Faced by failure of credit they have proposed only the lending of more money. Stripped of the lure of profit by which to induce our people to follow their false leadership, they have resorted to exhortations, pleading tearfully for restored confidence. They know only the rules of a generation of self-seekers. They have no vision, and when there is no vision, the people perish.

The money changers have fled from their high seats in the temple of our civilization. We may now restore that temple to the ancient truths. The measure of the restoration lies in the extent to which we apply social values more noble than mere monetary profit.

Happiness lies not in the mere possession of money; it lies in the joy of achievement, in the thrill of creative effort. The joy and moral stimulation of work no longer must be forgotten in the mad chase of evanescent profits. These dark days will be worth all they cost us if they teach us that our true destiny is not to be ministered unto but to minister to ourselves and our fellow man.

Recognition of the falsity of material wealth as the standard of success goes hand in hand with the abandonment of the false belief that public office and high political position are to be valued only by the standards of pride of place and personal profit; and there must be an end to a conduct in banking and in business which too often has given to a sacred trust the likeness of callous and selfish wrongdoing. Small wonder that confidence languishes, for it thrives only on honesty, on honor, on the sacredness of obligations, on faithful protection, on unselfish performance; without them it can not live.

Restoration calls, however, not for changes in ethics alone. This Nation asks for action, and action now.

Our greatest primary task is to put people to work. This is no unsolvable problem if we face it wisely and courageously. It can be accomplished in part by direct recruiting by the Government itself, treating the task as we would treat the emergency of a war, but at the same time, through this employment, accomplishing greatly needed projects to stimulate and reorganize the use of our natural resources.

Hand and hand with this we must frankly recognize the overbalance of population in our industrial centers and, by engaging on a national scale in a redistribution, endeavor to provide a better use of the land for those best fitted for the land. The task can be helped by definite efforts to raise the values of agricultural products and with this the power to purchase the output of our cities. It can be helped by preventing realistically the tragedy of the growing loss through foreclosure of our small homes and our farms. It can be helped by insistence that the Federal, State, and local governments act forthwith on the demand that their cost be drastically reduced. It can be helped by the unifying of relief activities which today are often scattered, uneconomical, and unequal. It can be helped by national planning for and supervision of all forms of transportation and communications and other utilities which have a definitely public character. There are many ways in which it can be helped, but it can never be helped merely by talking about it. We must act and act quickly.

Finally, in our progress toward a resumption of work we require two safeguards against a return of the evils of the old order; there must be a strict supervision of all banking and credits and investments; there must be an end to speculation with other peoples' money, and there must be provision for an adequate but sound currency.

These are the lines of attack. I shall presently urge upon a new Congress, in special session, detailed measures for their fulfillment, and I shall seek the immediate assistance of the several States.

Through this program of action we address ourselves to putting our own national house in order and making income balance outgo. Our international trade relations, though vastly important, are in point of time and necessity secondary to the establishment of a sound national economy. I favor as a practical policy the putting of first things first. I shall spare no effort to restore world trade by international economic readjustment, but the emergency at home can not wait on that accomplishment.

The basic thought that guides these specific means of national recovery is not narrowly nationalistic. It is the insistence, as a first consideration, upon the interdependence of the various elements in all parts of the United States--a recognition of the old and permanently important manifestation of the American spirit of the pioneer. It is the way to recovery. It is the immediate way. It is the strongest assurance that the recovery will endure.

In the field of world policy I would dedicate this Nation to the policy of the good neighbor--the neighbor who respects himself and, because he does so, respects the rights of others--the neighbor who respects his obligations and respects the sanctity of his agreements in and with a world of neighbors.

If I read the temper of our people correctly, we now realize as we have never realized before, our interdependence on each other; that we can not merely take but we must give as well; that if we are to go forward, we must move as a trained and loyal army willing to sacrifice for the good of a common discipline, because without such discipline no progress is made, no leadership becomes effective. We are, I know, ready and willing to submit our lives and property to such discipline, because it makes possible a leadership which aims at a larger good. This I propose to offer, pledging that the larger purposes will bind upon us all, as a sacred obligation with a unity of duty hitherto evoked only in time of armed strife.

With this pledge taken, I assume unhesitatingly the leadership of this great army of our people dedicated to a disciplined attack upon our common problems.

Action in this image and to this end is feasible under the form of government which we have inherited from our ancestors. Our Constitution is so simple and practical that it is possible always to meet extraordinary needs by changes in emphasis and arrangement without loss of essential form. That is why our constitutional system has proved itself the most superbly enduring political mechanism the modern world has produced. It has met every stress of vast expansion of territory, of foreign wars, of bitter internal strife, of world relations.

It is to be hoped that the normal balance of executive and legislative authority may be wholly adequate to meet the unprecedented task before us. But it may be that an unprecedented demand and need for undelayed action may call for temporary departure from that normal balance of public procedure.

I am prepared under my constitutional duty to recommend the measures that a stricken nation in the midst of a stricken world may require. These measures, or such other measures as the Congress may build out of its experience and wisdom, I shall seek, within my constitutional authority, to bring to speedy adoption.

But in the event that the Congress shall fail to take one of these two courses, and in the event that the national emergency is still critical, I shall not evade the clear course of duty that will then confront me. I shall ask the Congress for the one remaining instrument to meet the crisis--broad

Executive power to wage a war against the emergency, as great as the power that would be given to me if we were in fact invaded by a foreign foe.

For the trust reposed in me I will return the courage and the devotion that befit the time. I can do no less.

We face the arduous days that lie before us in the warm courage of national unity; with the clear consciousness of seeking old and precious moral values; with the clean satisfaction that comes from the stern performance of duty by old and young alike. We aim at the assurance of a rounded and permanent national life.

We do not distrust the future of essential democracy. The people of the United States have not failed. In their need they have registered a mandate that they want direct, vigorous action. They have asked for discipline and direction under leadership. They have made me the present instrument of their wishes. In the spirit of the gift I take it. In this dedication of a Nation we humbly ask the blessing of God. May He protect each and every one of us. May He guide me in the days to come."

–Franklin Delano Roosevelt
  March 4, 1933